WATERSID
In Bucking

Nick Corble

COUNTRYSIDE BOOKS

NEWBURY, BERKSHIRE

First published 2004
© Nick Corble 2004

All rights reserved.
No reproduction permitted without the prior
permission of the publisher:

COUNTRYSIDE BOOKS
3 Catherine Road
Newbury, Berkshire

To view our complete range of books,
please visit us at
www.countrysidebooks.co.uk

ISBN 1 85306 856 X

Designed by Graham Whiteman

Produced through MRM Associates Ltd., Reading
Typeset by Mac Style Ltd, Scarborough, N. Yorkshire
Printed by J.W. Arrowsmith Ltd., Bristol

Contents

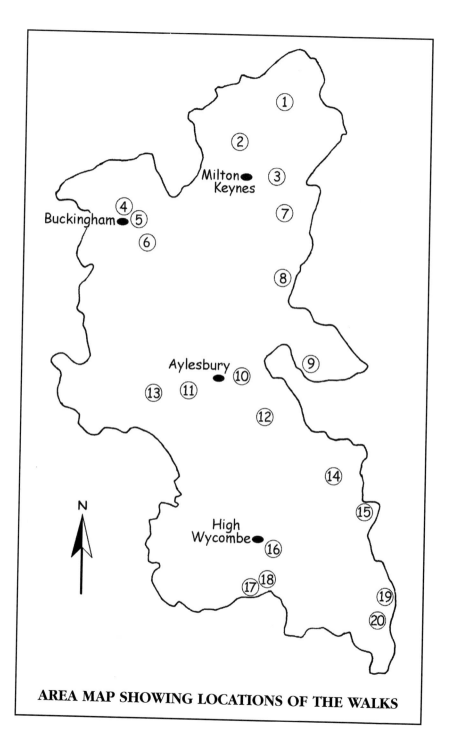

AREA MAP SHOWING LOCATIONS OF THE WALKS

PUBLISHER'S NOTE

We hope that you obtain considerable enjoyment from this book; great care has been taken in its preparation. Although at the time of publication all routes followed public rights of way or permitted paths, diversion orders can be made and permissions withdrawn.

We cannot, of course, be held responsible for such diversion orders and any inaccuracies in the text which might result from walkers trespassing on private property. We are anxious though that all details covering the walks and the pubs are kept up to date and would therefore welcome information from readers which would be relevant to future editions.

The simple sketch maps that accompany the walks in this book are based on notes made by the author whilst checking out the routes on the ground. However, for the benefit of a proper map, we do recommend that you purchase the relevant Ordnance Survey sheet covering your walk. The Ordnance Survey maps are widely available, especially through booksellers and local newsagents.

INTRODUCTION

A long, narrow county, three times as long as it is wide, Buckinghamshire's borders embrace a rich variety of landscapes and habitats. The north is marked by open heath and grassland and the majesty of the Great Ouse Valley, whilst below this the clay soils and grasslands of the Vale of Aylesbury effectively cut the county in two. Further south, the chalk of the Chiltern Hills provides the platform for a profusion of small streams and distinctive beech woods that in time give way to the Thames and its valley. Here, at its southern limit, peace gives way to suburbia as London's outskirts finally make their mark.

Buckinghamshire's waterways provide the perfect guide to explore this diversity. Firmly landlocked, Buckinghamshire can claim few waterways as its own, but this does not mean they are lacking. The walks in this book run alongside nine rivers, five lakes, six canals, and numerous anonymous small streams. The lakes are often man-made – the products of extraction industries over the years – and are now transformed as oases of pleasure, and, of course, the canals are man-made too.

Some of the canals, such as the Slough and Aylesbury arms, have remained in use, whilst others such as the Wendover and Buckinghamshire arms, became derelict and are now the subject of active restoration schemes. This relative neglect has worked in the walker's favour, with these waterways often offering the greatest variety of animal and plant life. Here patience can often be rewarded by the blue flash of a kingfisher or the surprise of a wild hare leaping into the air at the sound of your footsteps.

The Old Buckingham arm walk also offers an opportunity to absorb different phases of the county's history, including the Iron Age, Roman, and medieval periods, as well as more recent times. Then, of course, there is the modern experiment that is Milton Keynes, and the three walks featured here demonstrate that this city is more than concrete cows and shopping malls.

With the exception of the Chilterns, Buckinghamshire is not famed for its gradients, and, by definition, waterside walks tend to be relatively flat! As such, most of the excursions in this book are suitable for walkers of any age and also for families. Each of the walks is circular and offers suggestions on where refreshments can be gained as well as interesting places to visit nearby.

Given the nature of the walks, I have tried to feature a number of 'family friendly' attractions, although readers are advised to read the walks through first, as I have taken the opportunity to offer a range and to include some more challenging routes for experienced walkers. With rare exceptions, each of the walks has designated parking and many can be accessed by public transport. Each walk has a sketch map, but changes can take place and, despite the fact that all are well waymarked, I advise the use of the excellent Explorer range of OS maps and have given a starting grid reference for each walk.

As a long-time Buckinghamshire resident, writing this book has opened the county up for me. I have particularly enjoyed discovering the sweep of the early stages of the River Great Ouse in the north as it gathers up different tributaries to build its strength for the long journey to the Wash. In contrast, the chalk streams of the Chilterns make up for their relative lack of size with their dainty innocence and the unique habitats they provide. Watching a lazy brown trout hold water just below the surface of one of these streams can provide a good excuse to rest awhile – and a picnic a better one to linger longer.

Nearer the south of the county, the exuberance of the Wye as it is released from its culvert to the east of High Wycombe provides a good example of how an urban river should, and should not, be treated. Finally of course, there is the Thames, featured in two walks, with its variety of craft and idiosyncratic river folk.

I hope you enjoy these walks as much as I have and that they allow you, too, to gain a deeper appreciation of this often neglected county. I cannot finish without thanking my wife, Annette, whose occasional company on the walks and constant support has only added to the pleasure I have gained from writing this book.

Nick Corble

EMBERTON COUNTRY PARK AND THE GREAT OUSE

A gentle walk, taking in both fields and lakeside paths, as well as the opportunity to visit a historic village.

The River Great Ouse

The River Great Ouse cuts a majestic path across north Buckinghamshire and this walk allows you to appreciate it at its best. It also takes in Emberton Park, where four lakes created from old sand and gravel pits come together to provide a sanctuary of calm in the gap between Milton Keynes and Northampton.

Towards the end of the walk there is a chance to visit Olney, a market town which dates back to before Domesday Book. The imposing spire of the parish church of St Peter and St Paul provides a constant reference point as you stroll around. Olney has associations with the poet William Cowper and John Newton, a one-time slave owner and then curate of the church. Together these men wrote the celebrated Olney Hymns, which include *Amazing Grace* amongst their number. The musical connection is extended by the fact that the town has links with Henry Gauntlett, who is known as the father of English church music.

Since 1445, Olney has been home to an annual Shrove Tuesday pancake race, which more recently has attracted worldwide media attention. This is partly due to the fact that the race is 'twinned' with one in Liberal, Kansas, and there is an annual challenge between the women of the two towns to see who can make the fastest time.

Refreshment can be had at the Swan Inn in Olney, a good old-fashioned village pub, which also has a bistro. The pub offers an extensive menu and a wide range of beers, including Shepherd Neame, Fuller's, Adnams, and guest beers. Telephone: 01234 711111.

Alternatively, snacks and hot drinks can be had at the Willows Café in Emberton Country Park, although this is only open at the weekend and during school holidays between 1st April and 31st October. Telephone: 01234 711575.

- **HOW TO GET THERE:** Emberton Country Park lies a mile south of Olney, on the western side of the A509, 6 miles north of Newport Pagnell and junction 14 of the M1.
- **PARKING:** Car parking is available throughout the park, although a charge is levied.
- **LENGTH OF WALK:** 3 ³/₄ miles. Map: OS Explorer 207 (E), Newport Pagnell and Northampton South (GR 886502).

THE WALK

1. Starting by the Willows Café, turn right and bear right on reaching the water. Head down in the direction of the gatehouse where you came in and bear left, keeping beside the water known as Snipe Pool. A gap will appear between two lakes, with a boathouse at its limit. Cut across this and pick up the edge of the next lake, Heron Water. After 200 yards there is a gate on the right-hand perimeter of the park. Although not signed within the park as a public footpath, a sign on the other side of the gate confirms its status. Go through this onto a service road and follow this left to the busy A509. The imposing spire of St Peter and St Paul, Olney, will appear in the far distance and will become a constant companion throughout this part of the walk.

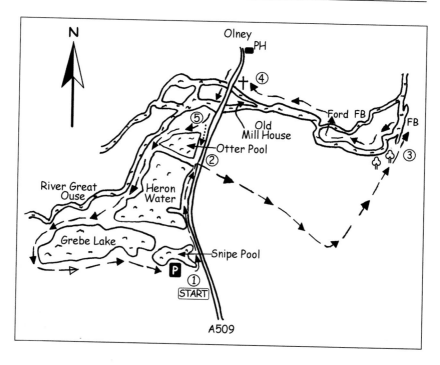

2. Cross over a bridge and pick up the footpath on the other side of the road, crossing into a field via a stile. Keep to the field's edge, with a hedge and small stream to your right. The footpath soon crosses this stream over a wooden bridge made out of railway sleepers, another characteristic of this walk! Continue to the end of this field and cross over into the next one at a stile placed slightly to the right, taking care not to fall into the ditch on the other side. Strike out half-right across this next field, aiming for the far right-hand corner. In the next field turn half left, crossing over some more railway sleepers two-thirds of the way across. The path begins to run over some rough grazing and becomes pretty indistinct at this point, but aim for the trees in the far top left-hand corner. Just before you reach this point you'll spot the path of the Great Ouse on your left and this should become your guide. One point in particular, near the trees, is extremely picturesque. Here the cattle sample the water and you can see the abundant birdlife, including swans and a variety of geese.

3. Go up and to the right of the trees and through a wooden gate. The path soon slopes down to the left and then crosses a series of

The Old Mill House can be seen from the route

footbridges where it becomes partially paved. When you have crossed the last, most substantial bridge, turn left and follow the river round until the church spire looms up before you once again. This is a very pretty spot, with the river wide but in places quite shallow. If the evidence of the anglers is anything to go by, it must also be rich in fish. Cross over an offshoot of the river, either by the ford or the footbridge further down on the right, and at the next field take the left of the two available paths. Keep the river on your left. Just before the path runs out, sandwiched between two mature willows, you can see Old Mill House and the reason for its name, although a modern garage now occupies the site. Back on the path, go through a gate and follow the road round to the church.

4. Cross through the churchyard until you come out at Bridge Street, where you should turn left, crossing the river and taking in a delightful view of the church. Alternatively, if you have time, pay a visit to pretty Olney stopping at the Swan Inn for refreshment. Back on the path, cross over another bridge; just before you reach a third bridge, the path slopes down to the right through a kissing gate and towards an avenue of trees.

5. This is Otter Pool, where you have a choice. Going left offers a short cut back to the gatehouse and your starting point. Going right provides a pleasant walk around the perimeter of the lakes, with a stretch early on where the path cuts through Heron Lake on your left and the Great Ouse on your right. If you choose this route, continue past the western limit of Heron Lake and along Grebe Lake until you reach a children's play area. Bear round to the left and past another play area until you return to the Willows Café and the start of the walk.

PLACES OF INTEREST NEARBY

Milton Keynes Museum, in Wolverton, follows the history of north Buckinghamshire and south Northamptonshire from 1800 to the present day. The accent here is firmly on items of everyday use, from telephones to transport and lighting to lawnmowers. Housed in a Victorian farmstead, the museum aims to appeal to every member of the family. It is open from Wednesday to Sunday from Easter to the end of October, and at the weekend out of season, although there are exceptions; so it is worth calling first. Telephone: 01908 316222.

LINFORD LAKES AND THE GREAT OUSE

A taste of the complex of lakes that make up Great Linford, coupled with the opportunity to sample the River Great Ouse in its unfettered glory.

Gifford Pond is a remnant of the Newport Pagnell Canal

Just north of Milton Keynes lies an amazing array of lakes through which the River Great Ouse winds unobtrusively, with the two often getting mixed up to the untrained eye. Out on the edge of the city, these lakes are often forgotten but they are worth making the extra effort to get to. Unlike some of the other lakes in Milton Keynes, the Linford Lakes retain the natural anarchy bestowed upon them by Mother Nature and these days are used mainly by anglers fishing for bream, roach, chub, and perch, as well as competition sized carp, catfish, and pike.

This walk incorporates a short stretch of the Grand Union Canal at the beginning, and also takes the opportunity to make a brief detour into a housing estate to trace the route of the disused Newport Pagnell Canal and observe its last vestige of water, as a small pool amongst the houses – a sort of contemporary village pond.

Often, on this walk, the water can be obscured by trees, but it is never far away, with local bird life advertising its proximity. The route is by and large flat and incorporates a variety of surfaces, making it more challenging than it may at first appear.

Not surprisingly, the Proud Perch in Great Linford has taken its name from the local pastime of fishing. This is a large modern pub priding itself on serving good British food, including sandwiches at lunchtime and meals throughout the day. It also specialises in wine over beer (mainly Bass). A particular feature of the pub is its raised wooden decking, which brings it up to canal level, and this is a perfect spot to sit and watch the world go by. Inside there is a variety of canal memorabilia including photographs from yesteryear. Telephone: 01908 398461.

- **HOW TO GET THERE:** Heading south, take the first road right off the A422, as it crosses the M1. At the T-Junction, turn left towards Great Linford, and the Proud Perch is on the left after ½ mile.
- **PARKING:** In the car park belonging to the Proud Perch pub.
- **LENGTH OF WALK:** 4 miles. Map: OS Explorer 207 (E), Newport Pagnell and Northampton South (GR 847422).

THE WALK

1. Join the canal towpath and turn left (east). Depending upon your direction, this point marks either the entrance to or the exit from the long twisting route of the canal through Milton Keynes, and the towpath is usually lined with boats. After the first bridge there's a long stretch of straight canal, and the bridge at its end marks the point where you will leave the towpath.

2. Just past bridge 77 (the site of Great Linford Wharf) opposite the turning point in the canal, there's a small alleyway. Take this and go right, past the old lock cottage, and right again. When you have passed a children's playground, go right again to Gifford Pond, a small remnant of the old Newport Pagnell Canal which used to join what was then called the Grand Junction waterway. Retrace your steps and when you reach the playground keep on the main road through the housing

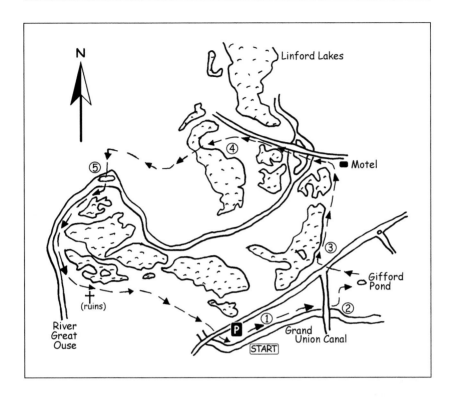

to a junction with the main road. Turn left and proceed along the verge to a point just before the road into Great Linford. The entrance to a public bridleway is on the opposite side of the road.

3. The bridleway leads to one of the larger of the Great Linford lakes, which often seem to merge into one another. At a junction of paths, head right and out into a grassed open space with a motel in the top right-hand corner. Head diagonally across this space to the motel service road and then left again onto the busier road ahead. This portion of the walk can be tricky; so take care walking alongside the traffic. You will pass over a number of bridges over the River Great Ouse until you reach a sign for Little Linford. Just past this, there is a footpath on the left which gives you the opportunity to leave the traffic behind.

4. Take the path on a raised bank that goes through the car park and across one of the lakes. After some woods you will emerge into open ground. Go straight ahead and slightly left, using the precisely

15

Linford Lake in all its natural beauty

demarcated footpath across a field. Pass over a series of stiles until you come onto a rough track. Again, the footpath is opposite, but this time heads slightly right. At the second field things open out, and you need to aim straight across towards the river ahead of you; when you reach it, go right, keeping the water on your left and passing through a gate. To your left is another gate and a footpath sign; take this path and follow the road it leads to. This then allows you to bridge the water at two points, the second having a small but attractive waterfall.

5. Follow the route of the small road. Keep with the road, passing the remains of an old church on your right. Eventually the road bears right towards some trees and follows a long straight path. Through the trees you re-emerge onto the canal towpath. Turn left back to the Proud Perch.

PLACES OF INTEREST NEARBY
Milton Keynes City Discovery Centre, further west down the A422 and close to the junction with the A5, is situated on the site of a medieval tithe barn and Bridewell Abbey, founded in 1154. There are substantial grounds, which visitors are free to walk round, as well as a welcoming tearoom. The centre offers a good insight into various aspects of pre-modern life, including fish ponds, a herb garden, and a Victorian copse. Telephone: 01908 227229.

THE THREE WATERWAYS WALK

*A flat and varied walk that goes past two lakes, a canal, and a river,
as well as a pagoda!*

A narrow boat glides beneath one of several bridges on this walk

If your image of Milton Keynes is one of roads and shopping centres,
this walk will change your mind. In fact, the planners who designed the
layout of the city placed a strong emphasis on the importance of water
and were at pains to develop a series of lakes, both to prevent the
possibility of urban sprawl and to provide leisure opportunities.

Willen Lake is a good example of this. One of two lakes covering
around 150 acres, this resource has become a haven for anglers, who
fish for bream, tench, and pike in the south lake and carp weighing 20
pounds or more in the north lake. The north lake boasts a watersports
centre as well as a waterski cable tow, a combination of wires and

17

pylons reminiscent of old tramways. There is also a bandstand, which offers brass band concerts on Sundays in summer, and a number of picnic tables. On top of all this, the Buddhist Peace Pagoda provides a unique attraction.

Pleasant though walking round a lake can be, it can become tedious after a while. This walk therefore takes advantage of the canal to the west of the lake and the River Ouzel on its eastern flank. These both provide a more intimate setting than the vast flat expanse of the lake, the latter also offering a dash of nature's chaos, in contrast to the man-made order of the canal and lake.

The Barge Inn is a large, traditional country pub offering Adnams beers and a range of food. The pub has a large garden and welcomes children. Telephone: 01908 208891.

Refreshment of a different kind is also available at the Camphill Café, near the start of the walk, although this is not open at weekends. Entering the café is like going into someone's front room, with book-lined walls, sofas and occasional tables. As well as hot and cold drinks and snacks (including cakes), the café sells home-made jams, pickles, and honey. There is also a selection of crafts on sale. Telephone: 01908 235000.

- **HOW TO GET THERE:** Take the A509 off the A5 in Milton Keynes and follow signs for Willen Park (not Willen Lake). Alternatively, approach via the A4146 from the east.
- **PARKING:** In the car park marked Peace Pagoda, north of the intersection of the H5 and V10, known as the Peace Pagoda roundabout.
- **LENGTH OF WALK:** 5 miles. Map: OS Explorer 192 (E), Buckingham and Milton Keynes. (GR 406874).

THE WALK

1. At the top end of the car park, follow the red cycle route towards the park. Opposite an information board about the pagoda, the path crosses a footbridge over the road. The Camphill Café is on your right, just after the bridge. In front of you is a bridge over the canal; do not go over. At this point you have a choice either to head down to the towpath or to follow the Canal Broadwalk, an avenue of trees lining a made-up path. Whatever your choice, follow the canal south. As elsewhere on the Grand Union Canal, occasional mile markers line the towpath, and soon there is one on your left indicating you are 34 miles from Braunston,

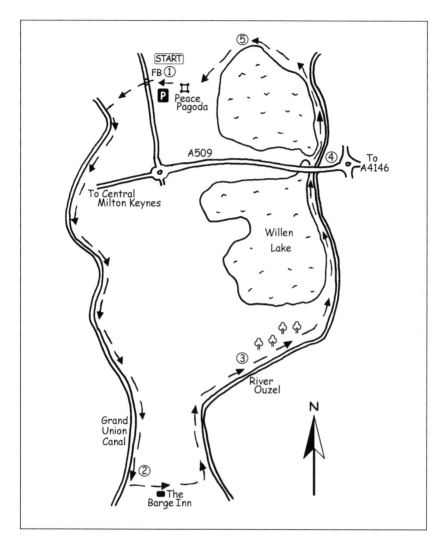

although it is not easy to read as it has been blacked out. Just before bridge 81B, the screaming you may hear is not that of frustrated walkers but of children enjoying themselves at Gulliver's World theme park, just visible through a hedge on the left.

2. Leave the canal at bridge 83 and join the path signed 'Riverside Walk and Ouzel Valley Walk'. Cross the road and continue straight ahead until you reach the Barge Inn. Keep the pub to your left and, where the path

19

The Peace Pagoda

forks at the end of the car park, bear right into the open parkland. At the next junction, where a tablet records that this was the location of a medieval moated site including ancient fishponds, turn left down to the river. This is the Ouzel, a gentle reed-banked river that flows unobtrusively round the outskirts of Milton Keynes and is one of its best-kept secrets.

3. Follow the route of the river for a mile or so, going under various foot and road bridges and into a wooded area. On first sight these woods don't look natural but it isn't until you get alongside them that you notice that, like the roads in this dynamic city, they have been set out in a grid pattern! When the trees end, the path bears left up a short steep hill, but the effort is soon rewarded with a fine view of the southern Willen Lake. This expanse is a haven for watersports, as well as home to a variety of wildlife, including majestic swans and a range of different gulls. One lake ends and another begins just after the A509. The weary can take a short cut home here by skirting the perimeter of the southern lake, but not much time is saved and the opportunity to view the Peace Pagoda would be lost.

4. As you join the northern lake, the Ouzel again comes alongside. The pagoda is just visible across the lake. At a kink in the lake near the weir is another archaeological site, this time marking Willen Mill. Indeed, the appearance of houses on the right marks the beginning of the small village of Willen, a place name which translates as 'at the willows'. Before the construction of the lake in the 1970s, this name would have been appropriate as the land hereabouts was a mass of twisting water banked by trees.

5. Follow the lake round its northern edge and then back down, using the pathway throughout. On approaching the steps to the Peace Pagoda, take care not to miss the board detailing the various types of wildlife to be found on the lake, which is a bird sanctuary. Examples include the golden plover, lapwing, snipe, and oystercatcher. Turn your back on the lake and take time to visit the Peace Pagoda itself and to interpret its wide-ranging symbolism. This was the first such pagoda in the Western hemisphere and was inaugurated in 1980. It contains relics of the Lord Buddha, presented by Nepal, Sri Lanka, and, somewhat bizarrely, Berlin. A thousand cherry trees and cedars have been planted around the site in remembrance of the victims of all wars. At the top of the hill there is a set of steps that leads you down to the car park.

PLACES OF INTEREST NEARBY

A useful bribe to get children to do this walk is to offer the chance to visit Gulliver's World theme park near the start/end of the walk. Aimed at those aged between two and 13, Gulliver's World has the fun of a theme park without some of the more brash elements usually associated with such places. Split into different areas, the park offers classic fairground-type attractions alongside some more adventurous track-based rides, the whole maintaining a pleasant innocence at a reasonable price. Telephone: 01925 444888.

CHACKMORE AND STOWE PARK

A steady walk that allows an unconventional approach to the splendours of Stowe Park and the chance to appreciate its landscaping from every angle.

One of the splendid lakes at Stowe Park

Although this walk can be completed in a couple of hours, it is best to allocate a good half a day in order to take advantage of the delights of Stowe Park, including the splendid sequence of lakes within. Stowe is the archetypal landscape garden and was the brainchild of the 18th-century radical Sir Richard (later Viscount) Cobham who conceived of building a garden as a living testament to his views on liberty. His aim in creating the gardens was no less than to record the history of Britain using buildings and landscape.

To get the best out of this walk therefore, it is essential to pause halfway through and visit the gardens. They are owned by the National

Trust, and there is a fee for non-members (call 01280 822850 for more details). In return, as well as the gardens, the Trust offers the usual facilities such as conveniences, information, and, not least, a tearoom. The park includes eight lakes, and when walking round it is impossible to move more than a few yards without bumping into some folly or monument.

The park is also home to Stowe School, the magnificent façade of which is also a feature of this walk. Back on the public footpath after leaving the park, the route takes you past Oxford Water and leads you to the grandeur of the Corinthian arch, half of which can be rented for holidays; the other half is the head gardener's home! Although the first part of the walk takes you through fields, the latter portion is mainly on metalled road and makes for easy walking.

The Queen's Head, in Chackmore, is located conveniently close to the car park and is unmissable with its white façade and cascade of hanging baskets in the summer. The pub offers an extensive menu, from light lunches to full restaurant meals, and the comprehensive ploughman's lunches are particularly recommended. Beers that can be enjoyed in the small garden or outside on the patio include Bass, Pedigree and Adnams. Telephone: 01280 813004.

Alternatively, there is a simple tearoom just inside Stowe Park, offering hot and cold drinks as well as sandwiches and home-made cakes. The ice creams and sorbets from the local Beechdean Dairy can also be tempting on a hot day.

- **HOW TO GET THERE:** Chackmore is a mile outside Buckingham, north of the A422, on the way to Brackley.
- **PARKING:** In the small car park behind the triangle of land before the pub.
- **LENGTH OF WALK:** 5 ¼ miles (excluding the Park). Map: OS Explorer 192 (W), Buckingham and Milton Keynes. (GR 358687).

THE WALK

1. From the car park, walk past the Queen's Head up Main Street and past the school on your right. On leaving the village, take the footpath on the left just after the road sign. Aim for the gate in the top right-hand corner of the field under an oak tree. On entering a fresh field take the path straight ahead, ignoring the one to the right. At the far end of the field there is a stile and plank bridge. Cross this and follow the right-hand boundary of the field you've just entered. Scarlet Pimpernel

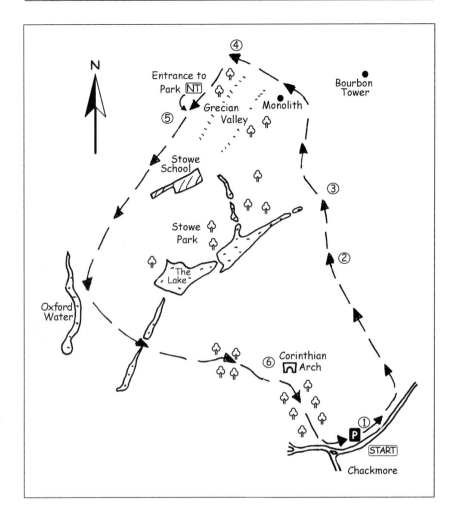

growing on the field edge contrasts with rusting farm machinery in the hedgerows.

2. On approaching a track you will receive your first views of Stoke Park in the distance. Go through the gate on your right and head diagonally (north-north-west) across the field, aiming for the gate ahead and using the red brick house on the hill ahead as a marker. This takes you under some telephone wires and through some short grass. The path goes through a gap in the hedge and out onto open fields once more. Continue in the same direction until there is a gap in the hedge

This Corinthian arch is passed on the route

on the edge of Stoke Park estate, which is marked by a brick wall. Go over the small stream that feeds into the lakes that form the centrepiece of this walk.

3. On approaching a gate, the path heads slightly left. You are now on National Trust property, but this is a public footpath. Head uphill, taking time to note the first of many monuments through the gaps in the hedge on your left. The Bourbon Tower is also visible on the hill to your right. This was built in the 1740s as a gatekeeper's lodge, with the octagonal tower added a hundred years later. Head uphill towards the monolith commemorating the Duke of Buckingham, moving away from the park's edge, and merge with another path, keeping the sports field to your right. Make for the gate ahead of you; this brings you out onto a long straight road, which it will come as no surprise to learn was a Roman road.

4. Turn left down this path, keeping the park's Grecian Valley to your left. The valley was one of the first major commissions of Lancelot 'Capability'

Brown, whose work is an essential component of any self-respecting landscape garden. The valley is overlooked by the Temple of Concorde and Victory. The official entrance to the park lies about a third of the way down this road, and the tearoom follows a short distance inside.

5. On exiting the park – or if you decide to leave a visit to another day – continue down the long straight road past the sward guarding the entrance to Stowe School. At the edge of the school's grounds the road forks. Take the left-hand path down towards a gate and a fingerpost pointing out over open ground. Oxford Water is clearly visible to the right, but the path twists away from it and between two of the park's eight lakes. Where the road divides slightly after this, take the right-hand fork and stay with it through some trees. At the end of this path lies the Corinthian arch and yet another monument. It is worth pausing here to take in the view of the park.

Leave the arch at your back and head downhill along the road. At the bend turn left, and you are back at the car park.

PLACES OF INTEREST NEARBY

If Stowe isn't enough to satisfy your desire for country houses, it is worth visiting Sulgrave Manor, the ancestral home of George Washington's family, bought on behalf of the British and American people as a tangible expression of the 'special relationship'. It lies in the village of Sulgrave, just off the B4525 road from Banbury to Northampton, and visitors are treated to a comprehensive tour. Sulgrave is also the headquarters of the Herb Society, and a large herb garden can be visited. The house is open only on summer afternoons, but it is worth making a date to see both the house and gardens and the George Washington Exhibition, as well as to sample the delights of the Buttery tearoom. It is advisable to phone ahead, as not surprisingly Sulgrave is often booked for private functions. Telephone: 01295 760205.

WALK 5

THE OLD BUCKINGHAM ARM

A varied walk that offers an insight into the different uses of water and land over the ages.

The Great River Ouse winds placidly through the meadows

Tucked away to the east of Buckingham is a concentration of historical curiosities ranging from the Iron Age, Roman and medieval periods to the early 19th century, all of which are included on this walk. The factor bringing them together is water, notably the confluence of Padbury Brook with the Great River Ouse, and later the canal.

The walk starts out near two tumuli or burial grounds from the second century AD, followed swiftly by the still visible site of a medieval village. On meeting the river, the walk takes you past Thornborough Mill and along the graceful Ouse until you reach the Old Buckingham arm of the Grand Union Canal. This arm was opened in 1801 and was officially closed in 1964.

Beyond a reservoir, also visible on the walk, lies an Iron Age earthwork, and at the end of the route is the glory of Thornborough Bridge, which claims to be the only surviving medieval bridge in the country. Apparently in the middle of nowhere, this impressive bridge provides a physical representation of the thriving settlement that must once have been, in contrast to the relative quiet of the area now.

The recently refurbished Lone Tree pub and restaurant, 150 yards up the A421, offers an extensive menu featuring English and continental dishes, as well as Greene King and local beers. The pub has a large beer garden, which overlooks views of the Ouse Valley and is dominated by a majestic willow. Telephone: 01280 812334.

- **HOW TO GET THERE:** Thornborough Bridge is 2 miles east of Buckingham, on the A421.
- **PARKING:** At Thornborough Bridge picnic area.
- **LENGTH OF WALK:** 5$\frac{3}{4}$ miles. Map: OS Explorer 192 (W), Buckingham and Milton Keynes (GR 730332).

THE WALK

1. Go through the kissing gate at the western end of the picnic area and strike out in a north-easterly direction to the left of the large earthworks. These are tumuli, or burial mounds. At the end of the field, go left along a narrow road and then right towards Lower Green Farm. Keep the farm on your right and go through the gate, heading for the kissing gate on the other side. The various undulations on your left are the remains of a medieval village, complete with pond. After the gate, follow a narrow path with brambles to the left, emerging eventually into a road with a T-junction near a stream. Turn left until you reach a footpath on the left near an electricity sub-station.

2. Head half-right across this field to a gap in the hedge ahead. Go right of the wooden fence in front of you and along the field boundary. When you reach some farm buildings, cross the yard and follow a concrete road to a point where it begins to bend right. The footpath heads left here, past a tree nursery. At the next field bear right and walk along the field edge, past a line of sloe bushes. Locate the easily missed stile in the corner of the field and cross an open area downhill towards a small red-tiled building. The grindstone in the courtyard is a good indicator of the purpose of this building, and sure enough on entering the drive you will

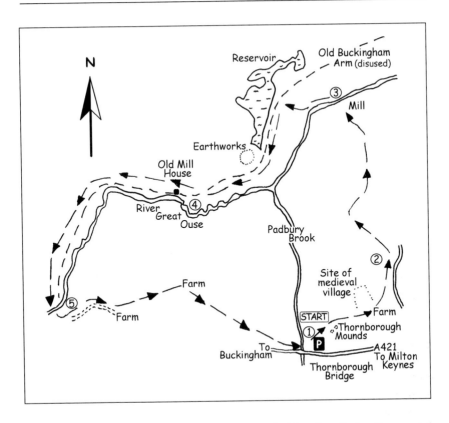

see a path over the Great River Ouse, guarded by the distinctive metal railings by Thornborough Mill.

3. Cross the river and turn left to walk alongside its banks, following the marked path. After a while, this sends you right, through a nature reserve and a small wood, to a plank bridge and over two fields linked by a precarious bridge. More woods follow, and another plank bridge. Just before the next bridge, bear left. A large reservoir becomes visible on the right and is your companion for a while as you emerge from the nature reserve and walk along a field to a disused pumping station.

4. Follow the path just to the left of this building along a field until you reach Old Mill House and a metalled road. Go straight ahead, ignoring the paths to the left going over the river. The path along this stretch is not always well defined, but it is there, just keep the river to the left until a kissing gate at a bend in the river, after which you pull up at a

Thornborough Bridge

bank and into open ground. Keep to the left edge of the field until you reach a stile. Keep going straight and once again you are following the old route of the canal, the towpath being clearly visible, as well as the results of some of the canal restorers' efforts.

5. At the next gate, turn left and follow the track, crossing the Great Ouse again. On reaching a farm road, turn left towards Manor Farm. Where the road bears right, take the footpath on the left, heading half right, and go through the gate on the other side of the road and across the next field, following a similar direction. Cross over into the next field and down to a gate and then diagonally over the field beyond, aiming for the farm on the hill on the right. Cross the stile in front of the farm and head half right; do not take the road. Go over the stile in the corner of the field and follow the path, turning further right in the direction of the road, back to the picnic spot.

PLACES OF INTEREST NEARBY

If this walk has given you a taste for history, it is worth visiting the Old Gaol Museum, where you can learn the story of Buckingham. The building is an early example of 18th century Gothic architecture. The original gaol was housed in the castle but, when the castle fell into ruin this new one was built. Telephone: 01280 823020.

PADBURY AND THE TWINS

A relatively flat and well marked route following a quintessentially English country stream and including just one small hill.

Oxland Bridge

Secreted away off the main road, Padbury could be said to offer a case study of English rural life, reminiscent of Ambridge, the fictional setting of *The Archers*. The housing is a mixture of modern, red-brick Victorian, and terraced farm cottages, with a liberal sprinkling of thatched homes, suggesting that the village has grown steadily over time. Although developed on a linear pattern, a number of farms line the side roads and evidence of their activity is never far away.

The village also gives its name to the local river, the Padbury Brook, which follows the contour of the land to create an elbow to the south and east of the village, which sits on a slight hill. The brook is the first of ten tributaries that feed into the River Great Ouse, which rises in Northamptonshire and grows in size and significance until it eventually flows into the Wash.

This walk traces the water's edge for a considerable distance, offering the opportunity to stop at any of a number of lovely spots, whether to eat a picnic or simply to admire the diversity of wildlife we are still lucky enough to have in our countryside. The water here is 'young', in that it twists and turns with the freedom of someone still finding their way, and its banks support a wide range of meadow-loving flora. Away from the water, parts of the walk can be tricky, however, depending on how thoroughly the fields have been cut, and may not be suitable for those unused or unwilling to negotiate high stinging nettles and thistles.

Padbury's answer to the Bull in Ambridge is the Blackbird. This is the very epitome of a local's pub, complete with photos of village football and cricket teams down the ages, as well as some of the numerous trophies local teams have won. The pub boasts a pool table, juke box, and fruit machine. The ceiling behind the bar is full of dangling tankards belonging to the regulars, of which there seem to be a few! The long bar supports a wide range of beers, lagers, and ciders, as well as a companionable clientele perched on their stools. Telephone: 01280 813017.

If food is not available at the Blackbird, an alternative pub is the New Inn on the A413. Telephone: 01280 813173.

- **HOW TO GET THERE:** Padbury lies on the A413 between Aylesbury and Buckingham, about 2 miles south-east of Buckingham. Take the local road into the village.
- **PARKING:** Anywhere in the village of Padbury.
- **LENGTH OF WALK:** $4^3/_4$ miles. Map: OS Explorer 192 (W), Buckingham and Milton Keynes (GR 715303).

THE WALK

1. Take the main road south out of Padbury to the triangle of grass at a junction, and head right (signed Buckingham) where the road bends away to the left. Head up to the bridge in the next bend. This is Oxlane Bridge and offers the first sight of Padbury Brook on this walk. Take the footpath immediately after the bridge on the left and cross the stream trickling into the brook. Having sighted the water, you immediately leave it, heading diagonally across the field towards the trees ahead. This brings you back to the brook, which suddenly and illogically reappears and now becomes your companion for the next mile, although it seems considerably longer.

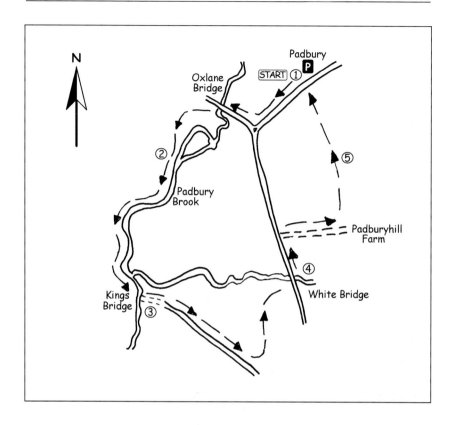

2. Take advantage of the gap in the bank to take a peek at the junction in the water that leads down to Padbury Mill, and on returning to the bank simply follow the water round, keeping it to your left as you echo its twisting course. The brook is known in these parts as The Twins, and one theory is that this is because of this fork, although another is that the name derives from the two tumuli a couple of miles to the north (see Walk 5). The brook is fairly substantial here, about 30 feet wide but quite shallow. The banks are lined with willows and rosebay willowherb, as well as reeds and, occasionally, tall walls of bamboo. Follow the well marked path and take advantage of the various bridges and stiles as they become available. Towards the end of the stretch, the water seems to divide, but don't panic; simply take the gap in the hedge to the right and rejoin it. A final stile brings you to King's Bridge, a functional steel and railway sleeper affair unbefitting its grand name.

3. The path joins the Cross Bucks Way here, but we don't keep with it for long. Go left over the bridge and onto a track which opens out into a minor road at Lower Kingsbridge Farm. Take a right turn, away from the farm, and follow the long straight section of road until just before it bends. Take the marked footpath and go through two fields, keeping the boundary to your left. Take care here, as the path is not well maintained, and there are hidden dips and ditches near the field edge. Cut across a third field, and you should just be able to make out the red brick of a bridge ahead of you. Cross two other fields linked by a plank bridge, the second of which is populated by rabbits and the occasional hare.

4. On emerging onto the road, turn left and cross White Bridge over the brook once again, which tumbles over a slight lip at this point, creating a pond. Follow the road for $1/_3$ mile north, taking care to avoid the traffic, to just before the brow of the hill, where the path turns right towards Padbury Hill Farm on a concrete road. Before reaching the farm, a bridleway is marked the other side of a six bar gate. Take this and head uphill, keeping the field boundary to your right.

5. On joining the next field, head half-left (north-north-west), cutting diagonally across until you join another field. Walk along the right-hand edge of this and another field until Padbury emerges in a slight dip on the left. Cross the stile in the corner by some stables and through the gate into some new housing. Follow this road out onto the main road through Padbury and back to your starting point.

PLACES OF INTEREST NEARBY

Claydon House, a National Trust property, lies in Middle Claydon, 13 miles north-west of Aylesbury and 3 miles south-west of Winslow on the A413, south of Padbury. It is well signed and is perhaps best known for its connections with Florence Nightingale, a regular visitor to the Verney family, who have lived here for nearly four centuries. There is more to Claydon than Nightingale, however, notably its use of 18th century rococo and chinoiserie decoration. There is a Chinese room and the grand stairs offer a fine example of parquetry. Telephone: 01296 730349. There is also a tearoom, although this is not owned by the National Trust, and a secondhand bookshop for those who like to browse. Telephone: 01296 730004.

WALK 7
CALDECOTTE LAKE AND A
STRETCH OF CANAL

An easy, mainly lakeside walk, with snatches of river and a stretch of canal.

The Caldecotte Arms

This easy walk starts and ends at Caldecotte Lake on the southern edge of Milton Keynes. The lake was excavated in the early 1980s from farmland on either side of the River Ouzel, with the idea of creating 'balancing lakes' to store excess rainwater and to prevent flooding in what was then the growing new town. These days the lake is equally valued as a leisure resource. The waterside wildlife consists mainly of geese, swans, and ducks, while fishermen try their luck in the river.

The lake is certainly vast, and in order to introduce some variety this walk also includes a stretch of the Grand Union Canal and takes every opportunity to pass alongside the River Ouzel itself. It is near here that the proposed Bedford and Milton Keynes waterway will link the Grand Union to the Great Ouse and eastern waterways. If built – and it looks increasingly likely that it will be – this will be the first new canal in the country for over a century and will be a testament to the enduring popularity of boating.

A short diversion at the end allows the walker to view the site of the ancient settlement of Caldecotte, after which the lake is named. Although there is actually little to see there beyond an open space, an informative display allows you to picture what life would have been like for prehistoric man in these parts. Not for nothing does Caldecotte translate as 'cold cottage(s)', as the flatlands of these parts would have lent themselves to an exposed setting.

The Caldecotte Arms is found down Lakeside Grove and it can't be missed, since it was built with a windmill as an integral feature; however, it can only be approached from the west. The pub advertises itself as a 'family pub' and is part of a national chain. As such, it provides few surprises but does offer the comfort of the familiar, such as an extensive children's play area, efficient food service, and a wide menu. The main beers are Theakstons, Directors, and John Smiths, although these are subject to change. The pub's lakeside setting also means it is a natural magnet for geese and small children bearing bread. Telephone: 01908 366188.

- **HOW TO GET THERE:** Caldecotte Lake is just off the A4146 near the junction with the A5 on the southern fringe of Milton Keynes.
- **PARKING:** In the car park by Caldecotte Lake signposted to Caldecotte Watersports Centre down Monellan Grove.
- **LENGTH OF WALK:** 4½ miles. Map: OS Explorer 192 (E), Buckingham and Milton Keynes (GR 891354).

THE WALK

1. From the car park cross a small wooden footbridge over a stream, which can barely be seen for the luxuriant growth of reeds. It is practically impossible to go wrong in the early stages of this walk, as all you have to do is follow the path round the perimeter of the lake, taking care to take the path closest to water whenever you are presented with a choice! This will take you round a large horseshoe with stone seating, which serves as a kind of aquatic amphitheatre and is fringed with housing that seems to suggest a contemporary response to the Royal

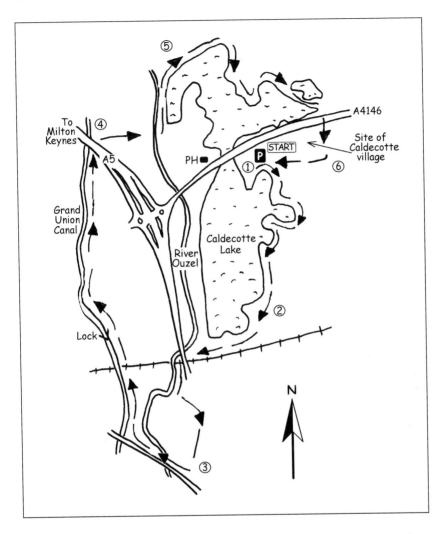

Crescent in Bath. This is followed by a second, smaller horseshoe without the terracing or housing. Shortly after this there is a series of jetties serving various watersports.

2. Near the corner of the lake, the path heads left and up, and then right, before going over another wooden footbridge. At a crossroads of paths, go straight on, leaving the lake to the right and office buildings (and then the railway) to the left. When the trees on the right run out and the lake is clearly visible, join the grass path on the left leading to

37

Caldecotte Lake

the road ahead. The road is crossed via a low underpass. Take the path to the left and go under the railway. The River Ouzel now pops up again on your right. Follow this path round to the left and soon to the right until it emerges onto a metalled road, which in turn leads you to the busy A4146.

3. On reaching the main road turn right and follow the path for ¼ mile, passing over the Ouzel once more. Just before The Bridge @ Fenny restaurant, cross over the road and down onto the canal footpath. Turn right and under bridge 96. The route now regains its simplicity, although it is worth pausing at Fenny Lock for two reasons: first it has a canalside pub, the Old Red Lion, and second because of the unusual feature of a swing bridge hanging right over the lock, which must make matters complicated. The Old Red Lion is a small, locals' pub, complete with horsebrasses and a TV, but is no less welcome for that.

4. At bridge 92 take the path up to the road and cross over into the road marked 'The Caldecotte Project' on a big green sign. Keep going straight ahead, following signs for the lake. Soon our old friend the Ouzel appears once more, but on this occasion it is channelled into concrete banks before regaining its natural state a few metres further on. The lake is now obvious in front of you, and the Caldecotte Arms is a feature of the skyline to the right. Just as inviting is the perimeter of this second half of the lake.

5. As before, simply follow the path nearest the water, cutting across the storm channel on its northern edge. Near the eastern edge of the lake, the path loops off and a small isolated section of the lake can be seen to the left, characterized by some vigorous bullrushes. Cross over a wooden footbridge and then another by a wooden pagoda before turning right. After crossing another footbridge, turn left into a grass track leading towards some housing, keeping the lake to your left. At the main road, turn left to go under it. Follow signs for Caldecotte Lake, going through a housing estate and a children's playground distinguished by stones arranged to look like a dinosaur skeleton. Keep to the red cycle path throughout this stretch.

6. At a raised bed with four trees in it, bear right, keeping the open expanse of field to your right. This marks the site of the medieval village of Caldecotte, and there is a useful information board. Pass another children's playground and cross the road ahead of you. Turning right brings you back to the cark park after a hundred yards or so.

Places of Interest Nearby
Nearby Bletchley Park gives the opportunity to delve into the fascinating history of early computers and how they were put to effect in cracking Nazi codes during the Second World War. In spartan surroundings and complete secrecy, 10,000 people worked at Bletchley during the war, and their efforts are said to have shortened the conflict by two years. As opening times are complicated, visitors are advised to call ahead. Telephone: 01908 640404.

SOULBURY THREE LOCKS AND THE OUZEL VALLEY

A walk combining canal and river and including a climb up to Great Brickhill to admire views of the valley.

The Three Locks with the eponymous pub in the background

This walk offers a combination of canal and river, with the two often running side by side. The starting point at the Three Locks pub is a haven for both boaters and walkers alike, as well as an extremely picturesque location, especially on a sunny day. The stretch of canal is typical of the Grand Union, being notably wide, as befits its status as the first viable freight route between London and Birmingham, and boats can still be seen which carry the livery of the Grand Union Carrying Company. It's also worth keeping an eye open for some of the double-width Thames barges, now usually converted into pleasure craft.

The canal's heyday was surprisingly short; less than 40 years after its completion, the railway had proved to be an overwhelming competitor. Not only could the railway carry bulk goods, but it could do so at speed. The presence of the railway is evident at the beginning of the walk, with express trains having a tendency to appear out of nowhere, often blowing their whistles as if determined to shock you out of your skin!

The towpath is usually populated by pleasurecraft. These are rarely moored up alone, leading to speculation that boating people tend to follow a herd instinct. They are certainly friendly and will nearly always return a greeting, whether they are moored or afloat. The locks themselves can prove to be a traffic bottleneck in the busy summer months, but all involved tend to wait patiently. Narrowboaters are rarely in a hurry. The River Ouzel meanders in and out of the walk. Over the centuries it has carved an impressive valley, which occupies the centre of the route.

The Three Locks pub marks both the beginning and end of the walk; so can be used to fortify the spirit or as a reward. The pub has an impressive wooden floor and low beamed ceilings. These features can make it seem like a cool haven on a hot day or a cosy retreat on a cold one. The pub prides itself on its good honest grub and serves Adnams and Bass beers as well as the usual range of other drinks. Once glasses have been charged, the canalside location is perfect for watching boaters negotiate their way through the locks. Telephone: 01525 270592.

- **HOW TO GET THERE:** The Three Locks pub is on the A4146, about 1 mile south of Stoke Hammond and 3 miles north of Linslade.
- **PARKING:** In the lay-by alongside the Three Locks.
- **LENGTH OF WALK:** $5^3/_4$ miles. Map OS Explorer 192 (E), Buckingham and Milton Keynes (GR 891282).

THE WALK

1. Start by walking away from the locks, heading north with the pub behind you and keeping to the towpath. Almost immediately there's evidence of the coexistence of the river and canal with a run off from the latter into the adjacent River Ouzel on the right bank. The path here is well defined – and flat, of course – making for easy walking. Soon, there's a ground-level mile marker on the left stating that the canal centre of Braunston is 42 miles away – a good three days boating!

2. At the first bridge, cross over and pick up the towpath once again, passing the old swingbridge, which looks like it's swung its last, and past

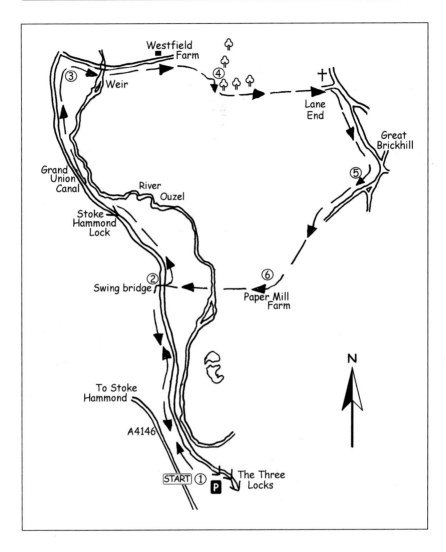

the pretty Stoke Hammond lock, which lowers the level of the canal by seven feet. The River Ouzel now comes alongside the canal, although it was never far away, and there is another run off into the river ten feet below. This provides an excellent demonstration of how canals hug the contour, so that locks and tunnels are only built as a matter of last resort.

3. Soon after the second mile-marker, leave the towpath just before bridge 102, going through a small gap and up some steps before turning

The Grand Union Canal at Soulbury

right onto a minor road. The walk now follows part of the Milton Keynes Boundary Walk, although the city seems a long way away. A trio of stone bridges takes you over branches of the Ouzel, and small weirs give the water a voice. Looking out from the third bridge, it is possible to see and hear a more significant waterfall. Opposite the drive to Westfield Farm take the footpath on the right and diagonally cross the field in front of you to the opposite boundary, and then walk alongside the Jubilee wood, planted in 2002.

4. Turn left in the corner of the field, keeping the derelict wall to your left. As the wall opens up into a disused entrance, bear right at the wooden fence, marked by a line of trees. Go over the stile at the apex of the field and up a narrow track. On reaching the road, turn left and then right at the war memorial. This is Lower Way. Take time to notice the curved wooden door in the house opposite. You are now in Great Brickhill. Keep on this road, past Chartwell Moor, keeping to the path until it runs out. It is here, on the right, that some expansive views of the Ouzel Valley can be seen through gaps in the housing.

5. Bear right at the Old Red Lion into Ivy Lane. Cromwell Cottages, an impressive row with their decorative thatched roofs, are on the opposite side of the road. Bear right almost immediately into Stoke Lane and join the public bridleway, keeping Broomhill House on the left. At Haines Farm follow the track to the left and downhill through some trees. Take care with your footing, as the descent is quite rapid here.

6. As you approach the bottom of the hill, the gurgling of water becomes louder. When you reach Paper Mill Farm, turn right into the unmade road. A small stream runs to your left and its destination soon becomes apparent as two bridges appear over the Ouzel. A modern house nestles on either side of the water, and unfortunately there is nowhere to stop and admire the view, other than from one of the bridges, but it is worth doing before tackling the final part of the walk. Luckily, this is easy, as this road leads you back to the bridge you crossed earlier when changing towpath over the canal. To return to the starting point, simply go back over the bridge and retrace your steps for about a mile.

PLACES OF INTEREST NEARBY

To the south-east of Great Brickhill, within easy reach of the A5, lies Stockgrove Country Park which is co-owned by Buckinghamshire and Bedfordshire County Councils and managed by the Greensand Trust. In a relatively small space (just over 80 acres), the park offers a wide variety of habitats, including ancient coppiced woodland, coniferous plantations, and heath. In these is a wide variety of native and non-native trees, as well as an oak woodland which has been designated a Site of Special Scientific Interest. There is also a lake, which was hand dug in the 19th century and is fed by natural springs. Telephone: 01525 237760.

MARSWORTH AND CHEDDINGTON ALONG THE GUC

This walk packs much into a short stretch of canal - locks, swingbridges, and a number of pubs - as well as the opportunity to sample life afloat yourself!

The Old Swan at Cheddington

This stretch of the Grand Union provides the perfect snapshot of all aspects of canal life. Marsworth and Bulbourne, south of the walk, are still working British Waterways yards, the latter being where the familiar black and white lock gates are made. The walk includes five locks and a swingbridge, as well as a congregation of pleasure craft and a boat offering cruises.

The banks are populated with both moored boats and anglers, young and old, who are after the abundant large carp hereabouts, many using nothing more sophisticated than chunks of bread as bait. This is a good spot to play the canal boat name game: challenge each other to find the corniest or silliest boat name. Equally, if you thought all canal boats are the same, look again. On this stretch you will find custom-made cruisers, converted butties, and double width Thames-style barges.

There are also some wonderful views to be had. Early in the walk you will see the mound of Beacon Hill, the site of Ivinghoe Beacon, on the right, as well as Dunstable Downs. There is also an opportunity to stray into the countryside to the west of the canal and to appreciate the variety of uses to which it is put.

As a glance at the description of this walk will show, there is no shortage of pubs to pause at en route. If your fancy is for the less predictable, however, why not try the Bluebell Tearooms in Marsworth (01442 891708). The service may be erratic and the atmosphere delightfully chaotic, but the home-made cakes, fresh coffee, and range of teas (including mango and elderflower) make for a delicious break. The tearooms also serve as an outlet for hand-made cards, a gallery for local artists, and a second-hand bookshop.

- **HOW TO GET THERE:** Head north on the B489 off the A41 at Aston Clinton. Go through Marsworth and turn left just before the railway line, following the signpost for canal cruises towards Cheddington.
- **PARKING:** Park in the car park on the left just after the canal bridge. The road over the bridge is controlled by traffic lights.
- **LENGTH OF WALK:** 5¼ miles. Map: OS Explorer 181, Chiltern Hills North (GR 927161).

THE WALK

1. From the car park turn left along the towpath and under bridge 126, past the wharf on the other bank, and under the railway bridge. You soon encounter a swing bridge, an unusual sight on the Grand Union, so be aware that boaters may be caught out and stopping to sort it out. This is followed by a lock and, in time, by another two, the three being known as the Seabrook Locks, which raise the canal by a total of 20 feet. You also pass a GUC mile-marker indicating that you are 52 miles from Braunston. Leave the canal at Ivinghoe Bridge (number 123) and turn left onto the road.

2. Follow the road until you find a footpath opposite some stables. Go over the stile and continue along the left-hand edge of this and the subsequent field, crossing the stile that connects them. The footpath in the second field cuts diagonally across the field to pass under the

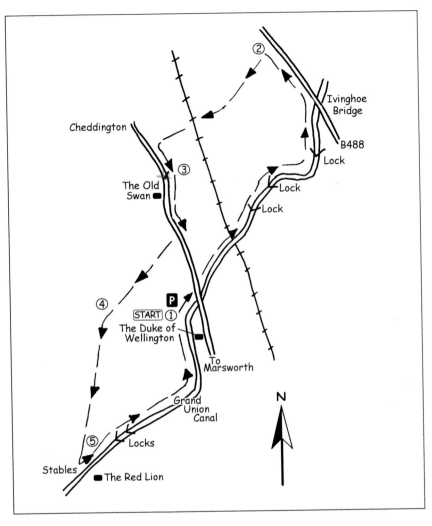

railway, and there are often cattle in this field so you may wish to exercise caution. After the railway, the path becomes well defined and leads you to a gate in the narrow end of the field amongst some houses. This is the edge of Cheddington, a small village so close to the county boundary that it has a Bedfordshire postcode. Having negotiated the gate, turn left on the path alongside the road.

3. Continue straight ahead, passing the Old Swan (01296 668226), a delightful thatched building that has been a pub for over 250 years. The

Ivinghoe Bridge on the Grand Union Canal

Old Swan serves food, real ale, and a range of wines. It also has a play area and large garden. Past the pub go downhill, passing some playing fields and Falcon House. The footpath resumes on the right, about ¹/₂ mile from the centre of the village and adjacent to a pumping station, which actually sits on top of a natural spring. If you look down the road you can see the canal, but be patient; you will be rejoining it further down. Follow the right-hand edge of the field here. It can become overgrown, in which case there is an option to follow the track on the other side of the hedge, accessed by a gap.

4. On reaching an open storage space, pick the track up again on the opposite side, past some trees, and follow it alongside a hedge. The track bends right, left, and then right again, before going through a gate and over a stream, which can be heard rather than seen. Turn right and at the fork bear left, following the main path. The track continues to twist and turn, but stick with it. Over on the far left, the distinctive black and white of a British Waterways lock can be seen alongside a lock-keeper's cottage. The track eventually emerges in a complex of stables, marked by a collection of horseboxes and trailers. Go through and join a road that takes you past a pair of very attractive canalside thatched cottages. Rejoin the towpath on the other side of the bridge.

5. If you go over the bridge (number 130) you will find the Red Lion (01296 668366), another pub just inside Buckinghamshire, this time with a Hertfordshire postcode! Here there is a restaurant and a wide selection of beers. Back on the towpath, go past a pair of locks and approach a grand grey timbered boathouse on the opposite bank that looks as if it might be more at home on Cape Cod than on the canal. If you're lucky, you may also spot white flecks circling in the air to your right – these are gliders coming off Dunstable Downs – or even a hot air balloon. Go past the bend the boathouse sits on and you will be back at the car park. If you have managed to resist the various pubs en route, there is a final temptation with the Duke of Wellington (01296 661402) over the bridge in Pitstone; this is another ancient hostelry (complete with beer garden) offering food and real ales.

PLACES OF INTEREST NEARBY

If watching the boats on the canals has given you a taste for trying it for yourself, trips are available from Grebe Canal Cruises (01296 661920) on the other side of the bridge from the car park at Pitstone Wharf. The company does both narrated cruises, lasting either one and a half or three hours (the latter includes a cream tea!), and day boats. Self-driven day boats can be a great way to find out if you are cut out for life afloat. These can take up to ten people and are small and easy to handle, as well as coming equipped with a basic galley and toilet facilities. Furthermore, if you head south, there is no shortage of places to stop and take on refreshment!

WALK 10

THE AYLESBURY ARM

A peaceful stroll along a canal that is something of an oddity on the Grand Union whilst taking in the surrounding countryside.

The peaceful Aylesbury Arm

The Aylesbury Arm was originally one of many spurs off the main arterial trunk of the then Grand Junction Canal, which later became part of the Grand Union. It was opened in 1815; $6\frac{1}{4}$ miles long, it linked the main part of the canal at Marsworth with the growing county centre that was Aylesbury. There are 16 locks along this short stretch, pulling the canal up a total of 95 feet. The canal was used for transporting heavy freight such as grain, coal, timber, and building materials and continued in use until the 1960s.

What makes this arm something of an oddity is that it is a narrow beam canal, despite the fact that the Grand Union is broad beam, i.e. capable of taking two boats side by side in its locks. Moreover, it is also extremely quiet, and this section has been described by some as the most peaceful stretch of canal in the country. Whether this is true or not it certainly offers good views of the surrounding countryside, some of which is explored in this walk.

The land hereabouts is flat, which makes for easy walking. There are some short stretches, however, where a good scythe might not go amiss, and some boaters may welcome such an implement when looking for somewhere to moor, since the banks are often covered with high bamboo creating an impenetrable curtain along the bank. Unsurprisingly, most boats seem to head straight for the terminus.

Refreshment is available at the Old Moat House in Broughton Crossing, over the bridge and further north from the car park. This is a traditional pub with a 40-seat restaurant and a large garden and car park. Home cooked food is served every day except Tuesday, when the pub is closed. Telephone: 01296 485228.

Alternatively, the tearoom at the Oak Farm Rare Breeds Park (see below) offers a selection of drinks, snacks, and ice cream.

- **HOW TO GET THERE:** Just beyond Broughton on a minor road heading north off the A41 east of Aylesbury. Follow the brown tourist signs for the Oak Farm Rare Breeds Centre.
- **PARKING:** At British Waterways' Broughton car park just before the canal bridge heading north.
- **LENGTH OF WALK:** 4¼ miles. Map: OS Explorer 181 Chiltern Hills North (GR 842142).

THE WALK

1. Head south down the main road, keeping the canal at your back. Enter Broughton proper and go past the attractive blue and white thatched cottage positioned sideways to the road and past the rare breeds centre and camp site, all on your left. Immediately after the last of these, there is a footpath on the left, marked unconventionally with a single white arrow on a green background. Cross the field ahead of you, keeping the boundary to your left and listening out for the strange noises emanating from the other side of the hedge. These belong to the animals from Oak Farm Rare Breeds Park. In the next field ignore the gap in the hedge on the left after about 30 yards. The path actually cuts diagonally across the field, but you may choose to stay at the edge, as the field is often full of cattle and discretion may be the better part of valour.

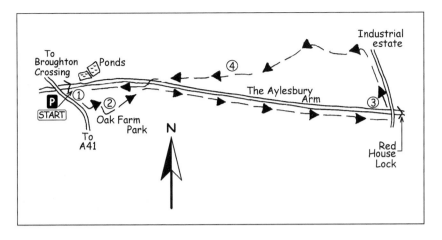

2. The footpath continues in the left-hand corner of the narrow end of the field over a stile. Take a half-left (north-east) path across a very large open space. The path itself is likely to be marked by tractor tracks. About halfway across, you will spot a red brick canal bridge, and at the end of the field there, as advertised, is the Aylesbury Arm. The towpath is reached by a pair of stiles and consists of well trodden gravel, making for easy walking. Cross under a series of farm bridges and the canal becomes extremely straight, like a Roman road. There is a bridge ahead, the portal of which seems to guard the gates of Red House Lock, your next landmark.

3. Come off the towpath and turn left over the bridge. Take the road up into an industrial estate. This ends with a rough track going straight on and you need to take this until it hits a T-junction, where you turn left. The going can be heavy here, but persevere, as flatter ground follows after a gate. Go through this and bear left, taking the path to the top left-hand side of the following field, where the route again becomes engulfed by trees for a short while. Go through a small gate and turn left again, skirting some grazing until you reach another gate just after a small stream. Head for the top right-hand corner of the following field and go through a metal gate, where once again the path becomes tree-lined.

4. Two more wooden gates follow, and it is just possible to make out the classic hump-back of a canal bridge across the final field. Head for this and cross over it to reach the canal once again. You are now back

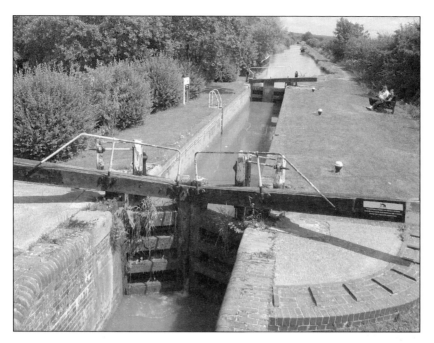

The Red House Lock on the Aylesbury Arm

on the Aylesbury Arm. Wander along the towpath for another $\frac{1}{2}$ mile until you spot some large ponds on the opposite side of the canal. These are the signal that you are nearly back at the starting point of the walk, and to confirm this the lock you didn't visit at the beginning reappears, as does the car park. On the other bank by the lock you can see the remains of a lock keeper's cottage that was demolished in the early 1900s.

PLACES OF INTEREST NEARBY
After having heard the intriguing sounds from Oak Farm Rare Breeds Park, it would be a shame not to visit. The park is open from Easter to October daily and charges very reasonable rates, although attractions may be cancelled in adverse weather, and it is worth phoning on ahead to see if there are any special events lined up. All the animals are named, and it is difficult to resist the temptation to buy bags of food to supplement their diet. As well as segmented areas, including a pets corner, rare sheep enclosure, and duck ponds, there's a picnic spot and playground. Telephone: 01296 415709.

STONE AND THE RIVER THAME

A delightful stroll amongst the lily pads of the Thame, taking in parts of Stone and the edge of Eythorpe Park. There is a short uphill portion at the end of the walk.

Weir Cottage on the River Thame

Stone is bisected by the A418, with the prettier part of the village lying south of the road. As the walk takes in the northern part of the village, those with extra energy may wish to take some time exploring the older portion separately, including the village pond tucked away behind the busy main road.

Eythorpe Park, lying on the opposite bank of the river, once belonged to the Dormer and Stanhope families, the latter having diverted the river Thame to create an ornamental lake. The estate was bought by the Rothschild family in the 1880s.

Man's interference on the landscape and the flow of the river is much in evidence along this walk. The water shows barely any current as it backs up into the lake, its surface dominated by lily pads, which provide a habitat for a range of wildlife.

The nearest pub, the Waggon and Horses, is slightly off the route but offers a good range of bar snacks, including pasties, as well as vegetarian specials and a short but tempting pudding menu. Beers include Burton and Greene King, and there is a small garden plentifully stocked with children's play equipment. The car park situated behind the petrol station is not large. Telephone: 01296 748740.

- **HOW TO GET THERE:** Stone sits on the A418 between Aylesbury and Thame, both of which are served by the Chiltern Line railway.
- **PARKING:** In the lay-by on the A418 near Stone village hall. Parking in Stone is confined to residential roads.
- **LENGTH OF WALK:** 4 miles. Map: OS Explorer 181, Chiltern Hills North (GR 785124).

THE WALK

1. Park in the lay-by on the northern side of the road going towards Aylesbury and take the footpath on your left that begins about 40 yards east of the village hall. The stile that takes you into the field is not easy to spot, but the footpath is clearly marked. Once in the field, aim for the stile to the left of the farm buildings straight ahead. Cross this and go to the bottom of the next field and over the obscured stile in the top right-hand corner. Follow the field boundary round to the right and, at a junction with another footpath, turn sharp left, taking care to ignore the stile that appears immediately in the gap in the hedge to your right.

2. You are now on the North Bucks Way. Head towards Waddon Hill Farm straight ahead, climbing slightly uphill. Keep the hedge on your right as you go round a corner, also to your right. Take care to ignore the misleading sign sending you over a gate, as this is not the designated footpath. On entering the farmyard, turn sharp left past the barns and follow the tractor path along the side of the field. The route now heads downhill and the River Thame can be spotted in fields on the right. Keep going straight ahead downhill until you cross the bed of a small stream along a line of trees; this may not be flowing in summer.

3. Strike out across the field now in front of you, initially taking a north westerly (slightly left) course until you reach the field's edge about halfway up its length and approach a small Western-bar type gate in the

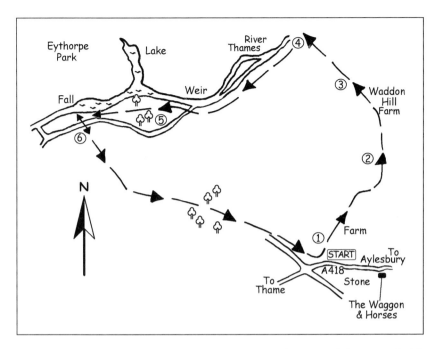

top left corner. Go through this and keep to the left of the next field, heading downhill until you reach the river, which appears unexpectedly.

4. Turn left and walk along the river's edge, taking time to enjoy its placid beauty. This stretch of water is in fact a subsidiary stream, the main course of the river being slightly beyond. On meeting a small tributary, either cross it, using the ridged plank bridge and climbing the wooden fence to do so, or take the easier path by diverting through the gate a few yards to the left. Keep the river to your right, ignoring the steep uphill path on your left. You soon come to a small weir, protected by the charming Weir Cottage. This is where the two arms of the river meet. On crossing the small bridge and emerging from the trees, the path briefly becomes a concrete road, diverging from the river for a while.

5. The road enters a small wood, where it becomes clear that the river has divided again as it is now on both sides of you, the more significant part being on your right. Emerging from the wood you reach a T-junction and will need to turn left. Before doing so, however, take a

A delightful stretch of the river seen en route

short detour towards the house on your right and a bridge that spans a modest ornamental waterfall backed up by a small lake.

6. Back on the road, cross the smaller tributary over a recently restored brick bridge. From here the walk involves staying on the road into Stone, going along the edge of some woods. This stretch involves a steady and persistent uphill climb that makes you appreciate the fall involved on the first half of the walk. As houses start to appear, so too does a path, allowing you to get off the road. One of the houses is a beautiful example of a thatched cottage, and even boasts a thatched roof over its well. On reaching the junction with the main road, turn left and rejoin the walk's starting point.

PLACES OF INTEREST NEARBY

Four miles from Stone lies magnificent Waddesdon Manor, which was built by Baron Ferdinand Rothschild in 1874 on top of Lodge Hill, which rises majestically out of the landscape. Waddesdon subsequently absorbed Eythrope Park. Now a National Trust property, the house is a French Renaissance-style chateau, and the gardens are currently being re-fashioned in their original Victorian style. Telephone: 01296 653226.

THE WENDOVER ARM

A quiet walk taking in a waterway that is part stream and part canal, as well as a haven for wildlife.

The George & Dragon, Wendover

The Wendover arm of the Grand Union Canal winds its way, largely invisibly, along its $6^3/_4$ mile course. No boat has cruised its length for over 100 years, but all that is set to change, for this stretch of largely derelict canal is the subject of one of the most advanced canal restoration projects in the country. This walk offers the opportunity to enjoy the benefits that have resulted from neglect - an abundance of flora and fauna. It should be interesting to revisit the walk in a few years time to gauge the difference regular traffic will undoubtedly make.

The canal was originally cut to provide a source of water to the Grand Union's summit at Tring, with the well head at Wendover providing a steady flow. At the same time, considerable commercial benefits were hoped for, not least the transport of live cattle into Smithfield. Its glory days were limited, though, with first the Aylesbury arm opening in competition and then the railways, but the canal's real nemesis was the fact that it had a serious leakage problem, which meant that in time it actually drained water from the Grand Union rather than fed it!

Restorers have already reopened a short stretch from the Grand Union and hope, with modern techniques, to solve the leakage problem. All being well, and pending sufficient funding, it may even be possible that the canal will once again reach Wendover within the next five to ten years.

The nearest refreshment is in the historic town of Wendover, a mile out of Halton. Over the road from the impressive tourist information centre located at the base of the clock tower is the George & Dragon, which has a friendly welcome as befits reputedly the oldest pub in Wendover. Despite being in the town centre, the pub still has the feel of a 'local', especially at lunchtime. Beers offered include Greene King IPA, Morland, and Fuller's and food from a varied menu is served until early evening. Telephone: 01296 625089.

- **HOW TO GET THERE:** Halton village lies north off the A4011 between Wendover and Tring. Turn into Chestnut Avenue – it is impossible to miss, as it is marked by a red and white jet parked outside RAF Halton.
- **PARKING:** In the village hall car park, just over the canal bridge down Old School Close, or on the street.
- **LENGTH OF WALK:** $4^3/_4$ miles. Map: OS Explorer 181 Chiltern Hills North (GR 873102).

THE WALK

1. Leaving Old School Close you will see Talisman Cottage in front of you, with reliefs depicting scenes of workers returning from a hard day in the fields. Turn right, and within 50 yards you will come to the canal bridge, by a white timbered house. Turn right, heading westwards along the well made-up towpath. The water here is wide and clean and it is possible to discern a flow. It has become a haven for wildlife here, so keep your eyes open for dragonflies and damselflies and the blue flash of a kingfisher, or listen for the distinctive cry of a moorhen. Pass Lower Farm on your right; the housing on the other bank soon gives way to woods. An unusual

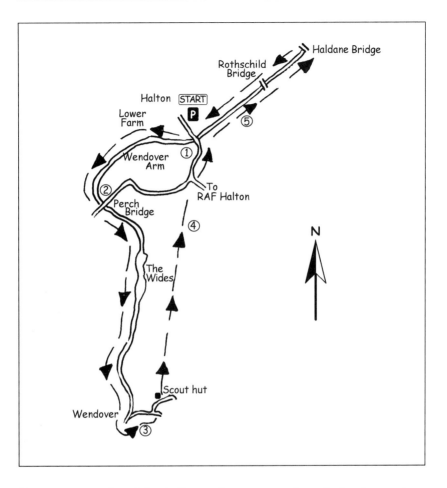

fingerpost on the right indicates by means of symbols that various refreshments are available a little under a mile away to the right.

2. You soon come to the distinctive Perch Bridge, an attractive construct of intricate white metalwork. As the canal bends, you enter a stretch known locally as The Wides, and it's easy to see why as the water spreads out. Originally the site of a spring that fed the River Thame, this spot provided a handy place for turning boats when it was incorporated into the canal. The vista on the opposite bank briefly opens up towards Wendover Woods and the path along this stretch is straight for ½ mile; towards the end of which is a narrow bridge marking the site of a disused railway. Shortly after this housing begins to reappear, signalling

The attractive Rothschild Bridge at Halton

the edge of Wendover. The towpath and canal end with a weir and a chain-link fence marking the site of a one-time wharf.

3. Turn left into the appropriately named Wharf Road, past the school and Wendover Memorial Hall, and then left again into Manor Crescent. Take the footpath on the left just after the Scout hut. After 30 yards of concrete, the path bears left over a stile and along the left-hand side of a field marked by a high hedge of apple trees and elder. The hedge gives way to a fence and at the corner of this the path strikes out half-right across the field. You are now walking across the open vista seen earlier in the walk. The path cuts left through a small wood and emerges into another field, which you also cross, maintaining the same direction. Beyond this lies some grazing, with some woods to the left and a danger sign warning of a deep bog – this is the other side of The Wides.

4. Aim for the avenue of trees to your right and follow this as it heads left. This path borders MOD property; so be sensitive to possible security concerns. Head for the white half-timbered houses where the path emerges onto a road. Go right here to a T-junction, and left into Halton village, marked by a wooden sign. The road goes slightly downhill and round a bend until you return to the point where you first joined the canal.

5. At this point turn right onto the south side of the water until you reach the impressive blue metalwork of Rothschild Bridge, which carries the family insignia. Baron Alfred de Rothschild would reputedly drive across it in a carriage pulled by zebra as he went round the grounds of his home in Halton Park. Continue along the towpath to the slightly less imposing Haldane Bridge and take the path up to the right and over the bridge, pausing to take in the view. The canal actually continues in water for another 2 miles to the east and is traversable all this way. The path continues for a short while along the other side of the canal but diverts into a field for a while before rejoining the towpath just before the other side of Rothschild Bridge. The towpath then continues to Halton village, where you rejoin the road and retrace your steps to the starting point.

PLACES OF INTEREST NEARBY
Five miles to the south of Wendover at Westcroft Stables in Speen is the Home of Rest for Horses. This institution goes back over 120 years and was created to provide a place of rest for working horses. It was created by a Miss Lindo, who was said to be inspired by the book *Black Beauty* and by the harsh treatment she witnessed being meted out to horses on London's streets. The centre is open every day except Christmas and the day of their AGM, from 2-4pm, and admission is free. Telephone: 01494 488464.

CUDDINGTON AND THE THAME VALLEY

An easy walk around the flat Thame Valley taking in the river and numerous small streams. The walk has one short modest uphill stretch.

St Nicholas' church at Nether Winchendon, and the unusual round pillarbox

The River Thame is a small but significant river in the local landscape. The river itself is often hidden from view but its course is traced by lines of willows along its banks. Although many are pollarded, others have been left to grow to their full height and sway majestically in the slightest breeze. Willow and poplar, another native tree found here in abundance, play host to a wide variety of birdlife, including reed warblers and cuckoos.

63

Although the main focus of this walk is the River Thame, opportunities to actually get alongside it are rare. There are, however, numerous small streams peppered along its route. Local geology has blessed the Thame Valley with many natural springs, which create short runs of water that pop up and then, equally suddenly, disappear. One such spring is sited near the beginning of the walk and creates a particularly picturesque scene.

The walk starts at the pretty village of Cuddington, tucked away behind the main road linking Thame and Aylesbury. Indeed, Cuddington has won the Buckinghamshire Best Kept Village award no less than seven times. Also featured is the charming village of Nether Winchendon, where the church of St Nicholas is well worth a visit.

The Crown in Cuddington is a grade 2 listed pub, with Fuller's beers on tap and an extensive wine list. Food is served, with an interesting selection of dishes on offer. Although there is a shop in Cuddington, its opening hours can be unpredictable, and no refreshment is available at Winchendon. Telephone: 01844 4292222.

- **HOW TO GET THERE:** Cuddington is $1/2$ mile off the A418, between Aylesbury and Thame. Both these towns have railway stations on the Chiltern Line.
- **PARKING:** On the road near the Cuddington Stores and Post Office. The local pub, the Crown, does not have a large car park.
- **LENGTH OF WALK:** $4^1/2$ miles. Map: OS Explorer 181, Chiltern Hills North (GR 737113).

THE WALK

1. Head into the heart of the village towards the school, keeping the church on your right. Where the road bends to the right, take a footpath called Tibby's Lane, which passes down the side of Tyringham Hall. This soon narrows and leads to a small pond and waterfall, the first of the many small brooks on this walk. An old well with a grill over its top and stone seating marks one of the local springs. Take the bridge over the waterfall and turn immediately right.

2. Follow this field down its right-hand edge and over a stile to a narrow path between fields. The earlier stream is now on your right but soon peters out. At the junction with another footpath, keep going straight along the edge of an open field. A line of willows on your right betrays the route of the fast approaching River Thame. At the bottom of

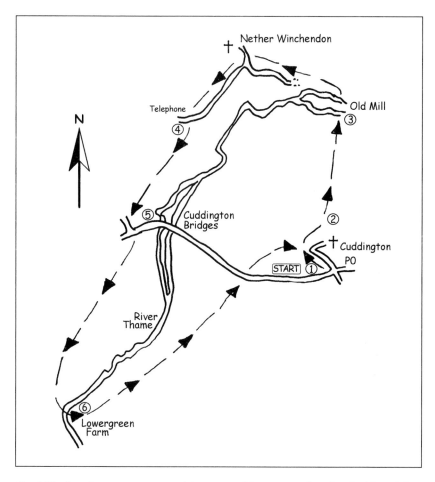

the hill, the river emerges and is crossed by a wooden footbridge. After pausing to admire the clear water and golden waterlilies, keep going along the edge of the field towards the stile in the bottom corner, taking advantage of the raised wooden walkway if it is muddy.

3. This stile leads to the Old Mill, with a proliferation of reeds on the left signalling the presence of a mill pond. Follow the driveway around to the left and pick up the metalled road. The route is marked here as the Bernwood Jubilee Way and is also part of the Thame Valley Walk. Woods on the left give way to the impressive walled garden of Nether Winchendon House, which sports particularly imposing brick chimneys. The walls lead you towards the centre of this pretty village,

The River Thame

where St Nicholas' church stands dominating the scene. In front of the church is an unusual circular stone postbox, inscribed *VR* for Victoria. Nether, or Lower, Winchendon, with its many coloured plastered cottages and unusual brickwork, is worth pausing a while to admire. The church itself has enclosed pews, a beamed ceiling, and a ground floor belfry.

4. The walk continues left, towards the phone box. Take time to stop and look behind you at the criss-cross brickwork of the Old Parsonage over the road. The path bears right at the corner of the field and continues straight ahead towards a road. Pollarded willows marking the course of the Thame are clearly visible on your left. On reaching the road, turn left and continue to a T-junction. The route goes over the road, but a 50 yard detour to the left takes you to the two Cuddington bridges and good views.

5. Back at the junction, cross the road and follow the right-hand side of the field, although the river flows along its left. In the corner is a stile leading to a bridge over yet another small stream. Cross this, keeping the stream to your left and ignoring the path across the open field. At the corner of the field follow the hedge to the right (losing the stream) until you reach a gap with another stile and small stream. Go over this and head straight on towards Lowergreen Farm through a series of fields. Go through the kissing gate at the end of these fields and along a narrow stretch with a wall on one side and young apple trees on the other. Go down the right-hand side of a cottage called Naleek along an ill-defined stretch of path, cutting diagonally across the field to a pair of stiles over another stream. Head over these towards the willows ahead and to your left, where there is another crossing point over the Thame.

6. Cross the river and turn left, walking alongside it. It is now possible to admire the river in all its glory, albeit for a short time only, as the path pulls away to the right. Head for the top left of this field, ignoring the alternative path on the right hand. The path is now slightly uphill, but not for long. By a cream coloured house is another stile taking you across a road. The path is well marked, even if the route itself can become overgrown. Head diagonally across this field towards some new cottages with very neat gardens. These lead to the pond at the beginning of the walk and from here you simply retrace your steps to the starting point.

PLACES OF INTEREST NEARBY

South of Stone in Terrick, the Chiltern Brewery sells seven bespoke bottled beers and brewery produce. The brewery claims to be the oldest working traditional brewery in the county and also houses the country's first 'Breweriana' museum. Tours can be arranged if you phone ahead. Telephone: 01296 613647. Nearby is the Bucks Goat Centre, said to have the most comprehensive collection of goat breeds in Britain. Visitors can feed the goats as well as other farmyard animals, an activity that is particularly popular with children. Telephone: 01296 612983.

CHESHAM AND THE RIVER CHESS

A gentle walk combining places of historical interest with the coming together of the various streams that form the River Chess.

A heron stands motionless on the banks of the River Chess

The River Chess is a chalk stream that rises up out of its underground aquifer just west of Chesham. This walk allows you to witness the birth of a river, from bubbling springs and widening tributaries, to their gradual absorption into a single waterway. For centuries, the Chess defined the local industry, with its beer-brewing, watercress beds and fish, all of which were sent up to London. There were also no less than ten mills along its short journey to the River Colne in Rickmansworth.

The building of these mills in turn necessitated some man-made intervention in the course of the river. Some of the small lakes created to feed the mills still survive and in more recent times became commercial watercress beds. Today, more modern tastes are met through the output of a bottling plant supplying water points for offices.

The walk starts at the Queen's Head, where one of the many tributaries to the Chess emerges as if from nowhere. The river is encountered along a number of points on the walk and becomes a constant companion along its second half, where it is possible to see a range of wildlife including herons and goose-stepping waders. The final stretch takes in some of the history of Chesham, which dates its first charter to 1257.

The Queen's Head is a traditional real ale pub, offering Brakspear, London Pride, and Fuller's ESB, as well as a range of lagers. The main bar even has a working piano in it, along with a collection of photographs of 19th century Chesham. There is a comprehensive selection of Thai bar snacks available, that are well worth trying. Telephone: 01494 778690.

- **HOW TO GET THERE:** Chesham is on the A416 north of Amersham. Take the B485 (signposted Great Missenden). The Queen's Head is on the corner with Water Lane.
- **PARKING:** Limited parking available at the Queen's Head; otherwise the Water Meadow car park in the town behind the pub.
- **LENGTH OF WALK:** $3^3/_4$ miles. Map: OS Explorer 181, Chiltern Hills North (GR 956014).

THE WALK

1. The river flows down the right side of the Queen's Head. Take the footpath through Wright's Meadow, where stood one of the ten mills that the Chess once supported. The path is effectively on top of the river, which then disappears under the approaching road. On reaching the road, turn right and head towards the King's Arms. Turn left into King Street and follow this round until the roundabout at the junction with the main road.

2. Cross over the road to the right of the roundabout. After 40 yards, take the footpath signed Millfields, passing the Christmas tree farm on your right. Bear left under the railway bridge, past the allotments, and along the residential road to a junction. Cross the road and walk along the side of the playing field ahead of you. Halfway up the field there is a gap leading down to a road through a six bar gate; take this and bear left.

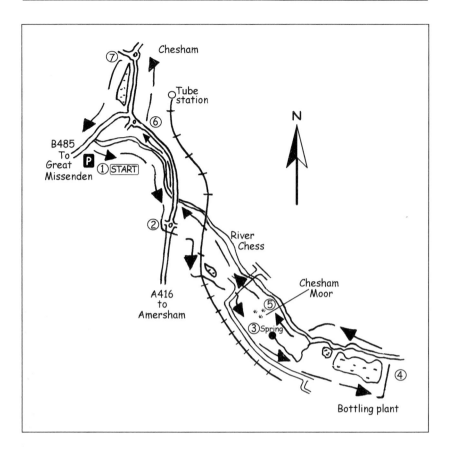

3. Continue on this road, which curves to the right and joins up with the railway high on an embankment, keeping to the left of the road. Just before the traffic lights on the brow of the hill go down an unmade road, where there is another footpath sign on the left. Take this and go down behind some houses. Turn right when you reach the road and head for the field straight ahead. Cross the field, heading slightly left where there is a gap in the hedge. Go through this and the metal kissing gate. You are now at the back of a water-bottling plant.

4. Follow the perimeter of the bottling plant round and cross over a steel bridge. After the bridge, bear left, keeping the river to your immediate left. At the site of Canon's Mill, where there is a small waterfall, cross the river and head in the same direction with the river now on your right. Eventually you will re-emerge on the opposite side of Chesham Moor.

5. Walk along the moor, beside the water, which is noticeably clearer here than its rather milky appearance earlier. Where the water forks at the corner of the field, turn left and over the concrete footbridge and then over the road onto Moor Road, the course of which marks the original route of the river. Go past the swimming pool and head right to rejoin the river. Do not go over the bridge, walking instead alongside the water and keeping it to your right. Continue around the back of Chesham until you meet the roundabout crossed earlier in the walk. Cross the main road to the right and go down the footpath on the left, following the same general direction, although the river is now on your left.

6. Follow the water until you reach the road, where you turn right and up into the town centre. Cross the busy main road using the pedestrian crossing and aim for the clock tower. Go up the pedestrianised High Street as far as the war memorial. Turn left into Blucher Street, heading towards the library and over the road into the park.

7. Walk along the side of the pleasant lake there and at the end take the path heading slightly right, which takes you through a gap to Bury Lane. On reaching the pavement, turn right and go past the old school house, taking care to note a number of historic buildings, including number 54, the oldest dwelling in Chesham, which boasts some 14th century wooden tracery. After about 200 yards you will arrive back at the Queen's Head.

PLACES OF INTEREST NEARBY

About 4 miles east of Chesham is Chenies Manor House. Built in the mid-15th century, it was at one time the residence of Sir John Russell (who became the first Earl of Bedford) and among those entertained there were both Henry VIII and Elizabeth I. The house is famous for its underground passages and priest's hole. There are beautiful gardens, including a physic garden and two mazes, and in spring the grounds are ablaze with a spectacular display of tulips. Home-made teas are available, but opening is limited to Wednesdays, Thursdays, and Bank Holidays, so call first. Telephone: 01494 762888.

THE MISBOURNE VALLEY FROM OLD AMERSHAM

A steady half-day's walk, with some hills in order get good views of the Misbourne Valley. The Misbourne itself offers a perfect example of a clear chalk stream.

The ford and footbridge across the River Misbourne, a perfect place for picnics

The Misbourne is a recent success story and a testament to the efforts of campaigners to rescue it. A natural chalk stream, it became a target for water companies because of its exceptionally pure water and by 1990 it was one of the 20 worst affected rivers in the country for abstraction. A new pipeline was built to supply the public from more sustainable sources, and it is now once again possible to enjoy the delights of this clear vigorous water.

The river first emerges above Great Missenden in the Chilterns Area of Outstanding Natural Beauty and flows for 17 miles to Denham, where it joins the River Colne (see Walk 19). The walk allows you to experience some of the benefits of the river's renaissance, such as bird and insect life, brown trout, and mint, sedge, water forget-me-not, and other waterside plants.

It begins in the pretty town of Old Amersham and heads up the side of the valley in order to appreciate some stunning views. The river is your companion for the second half of the walk, with a delightful stopping point by a ford suitable for picnics or a paddle. At the walk's end, a short detour can be taken to view the monument to seven Protestant martyrs burned at the stake in the 16th century.

Old Amersham has a number of historical pubs such as the King's Arms, which has a fine restaurant, although this is closed on Sunday evenings and Mondays. The pub has claims to be one of the oldest in England and featured as The Lucky Boatman in *Four Weddings and a Funeral*. Morrells Varsity and Tetleys are offered, as well as a guest beer, and the pub has a beer garden at the back. Telephone: 01494 726333.

- **HOW TO GET THERE:** Old Amerhsam is by-passed by the A413, about 4 miles north of Beaconsfield and 5 miles south of Berkhamsted. It should not be confused with nearby Amersham on the Hill, which offers a tube link.
- **PARKING:** Head for the large Tesco superstore and head west into old Amersham. There is a large car park behind the car showroom, with clean public conveniences.
- **LENGTH OF WALK:** 6 miles, excluding detours. Map: OS Explorer 172, Chiltern Hills East (GR 961972).

THE WALK

1. Walk back to the Tesco roundabout, crossing it diagonally. The path starts at Bury Farm, by a white house, and is clearly marked as the South Bucks Way. A short gravelled drive leads to a five-bar gate with a stile, after which you immediately enter a field at the back of one of the Misbourne's pumping stations. Keep the railings to your left and go under the A413 underpass, signed 'The Chiltern Way', following the track as it bears left.

2. You are now at the foot of a hill and on the right edge of a field. Follow this until you reach an opening in the hedge after 100 yards. Go

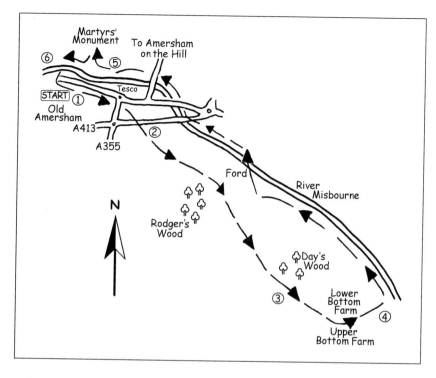

uphill, taking a south-easterly course and heading for Rodger's Wood, where there is a stile that takes you into the trees. This short track cuts off the corner of the wood, and you soon re-emerge into open fields. The route ahead is clearly visible, with Day's Wood offering a target. Just before this, go over a stile on the right-hand side and skirt the wood on its western edge. The trees obscure the valley for a while as you climb further uphill, again taking a south-easterly route, while heading slightly away from the wood in order to meet the next gate and stile at the end of the field.

3. Cross the stile and head for the gate in the bottom right of the field. The path here is poorly defined, but the gate is obvious enough. Go downhill, towards Upper Bottom Farm, going down the track where there is a short series of steps taking you to the farmyard. Turn left at the road, going past Lower Bottom Farm, which is in the traditional Chilterns style (i.e. brick and flint walls, with a storehouse supported on staddle stones). Before the end of the road there's a signpost where you turn left along the route marked 'South Bucks Way'. A line of willows clearly marks the course of the river on the right. The corner of the field offers the first glimpse of water, but the river quickly disappears from view again behind a wood. Continue along the edge of this and head straight out across the field when it ends.

4. After 200 yards there's an intersection with a track leading back to the farm. Head down the track towards the river, leaving the South Bucks Way. You soon reach a lovely spot, perfect for picnics or pooh-sticks, where you cross the river by the ford and wooden footbridge. The river now hides in a small dip, although it can still be heard. Keep the river to your left and go through a gap in the corner of the field. Go under the roadbridge and you emerge from the woods to see a sign for Ambers of Amersham in front. Head for this and cross the road just before it. The path goes past the front door of the Chequers pub, along Ambers' courtyard, and through a small snicket on the left. Cross the road onto a metalled cycleway, where the river re-emerges on your left, and continue along the path following the sign to Martyrs' Monument.

5. After 100 yards, the walk bears left at a second sign for the monument, but those who feel up to it can head up the hill to view the monument, a short, 150-yard detour. The monument was erected in 1931 to mark the sacrifice of seven Protestant martyrs burned at the stake nearby in the 16th century. Head back down the hill, taking care to take the path to the right and rejoining the walk at the second monument sign.

6. The cemetery is now on your right, and the car park at the beginning of the walk is on the other side of the river. Cross the wooden footbridge to return to the starting point. Alternatively, a stone bridge 50 yards later takes you to St Mary's churchyard, where the river finally disappears into a channel below an old building called The Lodge, marked as having been built in 1634. This represents an appropriate place to stop, but first turn left into Church Lane and take a look at the market hall. The walk's starting point is another hundred yards along the High Street to the left.

PLACES OF INTEREST NEARBY
John Milton's Cottage in Chalfont St Giles sheltered John Milton and his family from the plague in 1665. It was here that he finished *Paradise Lost* and started its sequel, *Paradise Regained*. The house is now a museum and is open to the public between March and October. Telephone: 01494 872313.

THE RIVER WYE

A gentle urban walk to discover a hidden river.

The Dyke is an attractive man-made lake

The River Wye in High Wycombe is an under-appreciated river, capable of surprising both visitor and local resident alike, for both its uncanny ability to disappear and reappear through the eastern half of the town and its pollution-free charm. West of the walk, it disappears altogether into a culvert that hides it completely from view until it re-emerges near West Wycombe, a situation which perhaps sums up the value placed on it by the local inhabitants.

Although much of this walk takes place in an industrial and built-up setting, it is easy at times to imagine oneself wandering through a meadow or small village. The river acts like a magnet for wildlife and is too small to be taken over by those who seek to use it for sport or recreation, giving it an independence that may go some way to explaining why it is so seemingly under-valued. The Wye is also in fact a network of streams east of the town, many of which are touched on this route. This walk may help to boost the reputation of this little gem.

The General Havelock pub, halfway round the walk, lies on the corner of Spring Lane, one of many road names on the route which give hints of what the area used to be like before it became built up. The building itself is an example of the characteristic brick and flint houses of the area. Owned by the brewers Fuller's, the pub offers hot and cold meals in a cosy 'locals' environment. Telephone: 01494 520391.

- **HOW TO GET THERE:** High Wycombe is 2 miles north-west of Junction 4 on the M40. The walk starts at The Rye, just east of the town, on the A40.
- **PARKING:** Follow signs to the Easton Street car park and the car park for the walk is 200 yards further east.
- **LENGTH OF WALK:** 4 miles. Map: OS Explorer 172 Chiltern Hills East (GR 870927).

THE WALK

1. The walk starts appropriately at Pann Mill, the last working watermill on the River Wye and only recently restored. Cross the bridge so that the open space known as the Rye is ahead of you. Head left towards the children's playground, passing through the gap between the playground and the river when you get there. On reaching a fence, do not cross the bridge on your left but rather turn right and follow the path skirting the trees. After about 30 yards, you pick up a stream as the path curves to the left, where it soon divides. The split is temporary, however, and soon the flow resumes a single course. Continue until you reach a small controlled weir and bear right, round the bowling green belonging to Bassetsbury Manor.

2. Pick up the concrete road leading you out of the park and turn right out of the driveway, following the road left until it forks. Take the left fork into Bowden Lane, at the end of which you will pick the river up again. Go under the railway bridge and bear left at the works, to go down a pathway with a small part of the river on your left. The path bears sharp right at this point, and you are forced to leave the river for a while. The path emerges onto a road which leads to a T-junction with Abbey Barn Road. Turn left and head towards the main road.

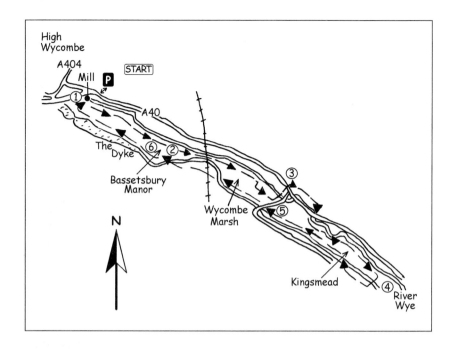

3. Turn right, and at Ford Street head for the path on the opposite side of the grass and walk down towards the war memorial. Cross the road and follow the path through an alleyway, where you once again pick up the river in an open area known as Kingsmead, a local wildlife conservation area. Keep the river to your left and the rugby pitches to your right, ducking through the willow branches. At the end of the open area, keep to the left, passing the entrance to Kingsmead Business Park, until you reach a wooden fence. Turn right and pick up the red cycle path round the side of the business park.

4. At a T-junction of paths, you encounter another stream, our companion on the homeward stretch. Turn right and ignore the small bridge over the river, following the sign for the town centre and keeping the stream to your left. You now emerge onto the other side of Kingsmead and can either stick to the path or walk alongside the stream. At the end of the open area the path leads over a bridge and up a small incline. Turn right on reaching the road, and the General Havelock is on your left. Turn right down Beech Road to see the old ford, and then head back to the road by the postbox.

The recently restored Pann Mill on the River Wye

5. Continue right until you reach the top of Abbey Barn Road and then bear left into the no through road until once more you meet the stream. Keep the water on your left until it curves to the right, and then continue straight ahead. Follow the bend to the right at Funges Farm. Just after Marsh Green Mill on your left, climb the short grass slope to meet up with the stream once more.

6. Keep the stream to your left until you reach a picturesque outflow cum waterfall. Climb the bank to the Dyke, a man-made lake, and the path will take you along the top of the Rye. Look out for the huge carp that live in the lake. Follow the path to the trees and then turn right, back to the mill and your starting point.

PLACES OF INTEREST NEARBY
High Wycombe was known for many years as a furniture centre, with chairs a speciality, the Windsor chair in particular. This heritage, along with the history of the area, is celebrated at Wycombe Museum, in Priory Avenue, near the station. Many of the displays are hands-on, and the museum itself is housed in an 18th century house. Of particular interest is the display of 'bodging', the ancient art of wood-turning using man-powered tools. Telephone: 01494 421895.

TWO THAMES LOCKS

An easy wander alongside a stretch of Old Father Thames between two locks.

Marlow

Marlow is an attractive and prosperous looking market town with much to be proud of and a lack of inhibition in proclaiming its heritage. Its location on the bank of the Thames and its position as a natural fording point for the road between High Wycombe and Reading means it has a long history, stretching back as far as the Vikings. In more recent times it has developed an association with sport, notably rowing, helped to a large degree by the efforts of local hero Sir Steven Redgrave, who went to school and practised here. Bisham Abbey, which is visible from the walk, specialises in tennis and rowing, and is occasional host to the England football team.

This walk offers the opportunity to see how river and town combine together along a stretch between the two Thames locks of Temple and Marlow. Alongside each you can see the weirs that make the locks necessary and perhaps contemplate how, until relatively recently, boats were forced to rush these mini-waterfalls in order to progress down the river.

The walk starts and finishes in Higginson Park, which also boasts a modern mosaic maze. Behind the maze, near the café, is a statue to the town's most famous modern son, his five Olympic gold medals draped proudly on his chest.

There are plenty of opportunities for refreshment on the walk. Light snacks are available at Temple Lock in the summer, and the Garden Café Bar in the park offers morning coffee, lunches, afternoon teas, and bar snacks. Telephone: 01628 405200.

Those preferring pub grub can choose the George and Dragon in the High Street, part of a chain of 'family pubs' offering a comprehensive menu as well as John Smiths, IPA, and Banks beers. Telephone: 01628 483887.

- **HOW TO GET THERE:** Marlow lies just off the A404, between High Wycombe and Maidenhead. On entering the town, follow signs for the Court Gardens Leisure Complex and tourist information centre. Marlow is also accessible by rail.
- **PARKING:** The Court Gardens Leisure Complex.
- **LENGTH OF WALK:** 4 miles. Map: OS Explorer 172, Chiltern Hills East (GR 848861).

THE WALK

1. From the car park, follow signs for the Thames towpath, although the river, which is directly in front of you, is impossible to miss! On reaching the water, turn right and follow the river upstream, going across a footbridge over a small stream until you reach open land on your right. Go over two arched footbridges over further streams and past a sign for Pen's Place. On the opposite bank you can see Bisham Abbey.

2. Go through a couple of gates into open countryside, pausing after the first to take in the magnificent vista of the river and to observe the variety of craft that ply the water here. Keep going past the monument to Giles Every and his wife, Bridget, the former a one-time secretary and treasurer of the Marlow Regatta. Shortly after this, the footpath offers a

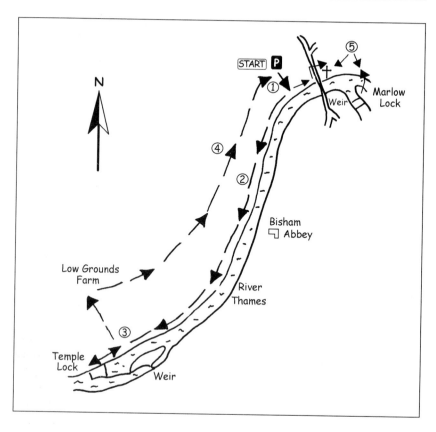

diversion to the right. Although you will be taking this path, for the moment continue straight ahead to Temple Lock, where in the summer months it is possible to buy drinks and simple snacks.

3. On leaving the lock, retrace your steps to where the footpath forked and follow the tarmac road, which is now on your left, flanked on one side by a high hedge and on the other by an open field. After about ¼ mile, just before Low Grounds Farm, follow the footpath as it turns right by some trees. This starts as a well-defined track but soon peters out. The track is a favourite route for cyclists and joggers, so beware. The end of the track is marked by a rusty padlocked gate, beyond which the path briefly enters some woodland before becoming a road once again. This is Pen's Place, highlighted earlier in the walk. Go past the houses, crossing a concrete bridge that goes over one of the streams flowing into the river.

4. Ignore the path as it bends to the right and cross another of the streams seen near the beginning of the walk, until you reach a gap in the hedge. Go through this onto a football pitch, and ahead of you is the river once again. Go to the left of the goal and back towards Court Gardens into Higginson Park, skirting the cricket pitch on your left. Head back towards the river, passing the Marlow Millennium Maze and the statue to Steven Redgrave on your left. Back alongside the river keep the water to your right, and on reaching the bridge turn left into the High Street, which you should cross. The George and Dragon pub is ahead and to the right, but before then, by the church, the path turns right and after crossing the churchyard is channelled between two high brick walls. In the churchyard look out for the lampposts with the heraldic chained swans.

5. At the T-junction opposite Red Brick House, turn right and rejoin the river. A sign opposite the appropriately named Lock House directs you right towards Marlow Lock over a wooden hump-back bridge. This brings you to the second lock of the walk, which is guarded by the magnificent sweep of Marlow Weir, and at the end of this is the renowned Compleat Angler Hotel, famous for its connections with the author Izaak Walton. Just below the weir, where now there is modern housing, used to be Marlow Mills, which produced flour from local grain and paper from rags shipped up from London by barge. Having taken in the view, retrace your steps to the church and cross the road, where you will find yourself facing another entrance to the park and the opportunity to take refreshment at the Garden Café Bar before heading home.

PLACES OF INTEREST NEARBY

Just outside Marlow is the Thames Valley Falconry and Conservation Centre, which is home to various birds of prey ranging from owls and eagles to hawks and falcons. The centre's founders have built up the collection and regularly give flying displays of the birds. It is also possible to arrange personal bird handling experiences and falconry courses. The centre is open from March to October and can be found in the Wyevale Garden Centre in Pump Lane South, near Little Marlow. Telephone: 01628 891085.

LITTLE MARLOW AND THE THAMES TOWPATH

A mix of rural and urban walking taking in both the Thames and local lakes.

The wide expanse of the river, with Bourne End glimpsed in the distance

The River Thames doesn't really need an introduction but if it did, this walk would provide a good one. The walk starts in Little Marlow, near some of the lakes created from gravel working, and sweeps down through the outskirts of Marlow itself towards Marlow Lock. Although a detour is required to see the lock this is worth doing if only to observe the organisational skills of the lock-keepers.

A long stretch of the river follows, with plenty of opportunity to spot the variety of craft plying the water, as well as the eclectic range of architectural styles employed by the owners of properties on the opposite bank. The river actually acts as the county boundary, and the contrast between the Buckinghamshire and Berkshire banks is marked, with the former including open public spaces and the latter much more exclusive!

Two large islands in the middle of the river add to the mix. One is used as a Scouting watersports centre, with canoes and small sailing craft a common sight, as well as Chinese dragon boats, whilst the other is altogether more select. On leaving the river, the walk skirts Spade Oak Lake, which in 1996 was declared a nature reserve, largely on the basis of the wide range of bird species which have made it their home. The walk goes on to include some small streams.

For those seeking refreshment, the Queen's Head at the start of the walk in Little Marlow is a beautiful countryside pub tucked down a dead end. Inside there's a collection of cricketing memorabilia, including miniature bats commemorating tours by the Little Marlow Cricket Club as well as signed bats from test match sides. Beers include Greene King IPA, Charles Wells Bombardier, and Tetleys. There is an extensive menu, with food served in either of the two bars or in the pretty front area, where it's easy to imagine yourself having a drink in someone's front garden – which of course you are! Telephone: 01628 482927.

- **HOW TO GET THERE:** Little Marlow lies $\frac{1}{2}$ mile south of the A4155, between Marlow and Bourne End, 1 mile east of the junction with the A404. The walk can be accessed from Marlow, which has a railway station.
- **PARKING:** There is plenty of on-street parking in Little Marlow, or you could park at the Queen's Head with the landlord's permission.
- **LENGTH OF WALK:** $5\frac{1}{2}$ miles. Map: OS Explorer 172, Chiltern Hills East (GR 873880).

THE WALK

1. The Queen's Head is at the end of Pounds Lane, halfway down the main road through the village, and is well signed. This is also where the walk starts, down a footpath to the right of the gate before the road turns into the pub car park. Follow this well defined but narrow track, which soon opens out into a rural landscape. Go straight across a minor road and across two more a few hundred yards later, which are the entrance to and exit from Westhorpe House. This area is marked by a number of old gravel pits which have since become lakes, and you soon find yourself walking alongside one of these. A better view can be had

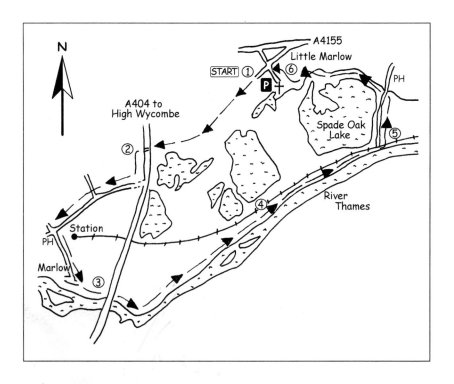

of the water by taking the path on the other side of the high hedge. When the path forks, bear right and cross the busy A404 by a metal footbridge, where there is a good view of the lake.

2. On the other side of the road, take the path immediately to your right, keeping the wooden fence alongside. After 100 yards, the path bends to the right and enters some housing. A small stream now accompanies the path, but unfortunately seems to be used as a local rubbish tip. On reaching a clearing, take the path on your left. At the junction go down Dedmere Road, slightly to the left. You are now in the heart of some housing. At the Marlow Donkey pub turn left down Lock Road, which, unsurprisingly, will lead you to the river, though not to the lock, which is a little bit further down. The railway station is over to your left. At the end of the road bear right and then left into some parkland to join the Thames towpath.

3. Boats can usually be seen on the moorings here and their owners are often ready to chat. Follow the towpath and take time to observe the

One of the many interesting houses to be seen along the banks of the River Thames

variety of buildings on the opposite bank. Within a few hundred yards it is possible to see a castle, a mock-Tudor mansion, a thatched cottage, and a Swiss chalet! The houses disappear for a while, the view obstructed by an island in the middle of the river which houses a water sports centre for local scouts and others. As well as the variety of housing, the river displays a range of craft, from Thames skiffs to cruisers, narrowboats, and sailing boats.

4. Continue along the path, past another longer island, and through fields, some of which may be occupied by cattle. After a little under 2 miles, you enter Spade Oak Meadow, which is maintained by Buckinghamshire County Council. On emerging from the meadow, you can see the massed masts of boats moored at Bourne End. The walk, however, bears left at this point over the level crossing. This stretch of railway may seem quiet but it is still very much in use; so take care.

5. Take the road into Abbotsbrook to the Spade Oak pub. Just after the pub, take the footpath on the left, going over a field and crossing the small stream at the end on the wooden footbridge provided. At the junction turn right, but look to the left, where the vast expanse of Spade Oak Lake comes into view, with its rush-lined banks. Ignore the still-active extraction work going on and take time to appreciate the lake. It is still owned by the gravel company, but the paths have been made public rights of way. Follow the lake round its edge until the path forks at one corner, where you bear right into the trees.

6. Take the footbridge over the stream and head up to the wood's perimeter. Turn left at the fence and walk across the minor road ahead. Another stream appears, and you need to keep this to your left for about 200 yards before crossing over on a wooden bridge, so that the stream is then on your right. Bear right and right again, effectively doing three sides of a square, before reaching a stile into a road. Follow the road up to St John the Baptist church and you are back in the heart of Little Marlow.

PLACES OF INTEREST NEARBY

Cliveden, about 5 miles south-east of Marlow at Taplow off the A404, is perhaps best known for its role in the Profumo political scandal in the 1960s. Once the home of Nancy, Lady Astor, the house and gardens are now owned by the National Trust. There are panoramic views of the Thames from the cliff-top location, and, although the house is now a very exclusive hotel, the public gardens offer much, including a series of themed areas and an octagonal temple with a mosaic interior. Some parts of the property can be viewed on certain days and it is worth phoning first. Telephone: 01494 755562.

DENHAM AND THE COLNE VALLEY

A moderately demanding walk amongst the last piece of countryside on the west side of London.

The Swan and Bottle on the Grand Union Canal

Denham is perhaps the last outpost of Shire England before London's sprawl becomes all-pervading. This walk describes a circle around the beginning of the M40, with the sound of rubber on asphalt providing a steady background as you work your way round. Don't let that put you off, though, for the walk also provides an excellent way of appreciating this protected area and how it has used its largely rural surroundings to its advantage.

The remnants of market gardens and nurseries are scattered around the walk as a reminder of how for centuries this area supplied fresh fruit and flowers to London. Its rivers also supplied water to the growing capital and a means of transporting goods into the heart of the city. The area's tranquillity has also proved to be a magnet for city dwellers looking for fresh air. Early in the last century it was a favoured spot for cyclists, and today many people still flock to the nature reserves around the Colne Valley and surrounding area.

There are a number of opportunities for refreshment on the walk. The visitor's centre where the walk begins provides hot and cold drinks and a selection of snacks. Telephone: 01895 833375.

More substantial sustenance can be found at the Swan and Bottle on the Grand Union Canal, including both bar snacks and a very comprehensive menu, as well as Fuller's and Morland beers. A 17th century building sandwiched between more modern architecture, the pub has hosted Stuarts, bargees and London cyclists, although these days besuited business folk tend to dominate. Telephone: 01895 234047.

Early in the walk there is Fran's Tea Rooms by Denham Deep Lock.

- **HOW TO GET THERE:** The walk starts at the Colne Valley Park Visitor's Centre about $\frac{1}{2}$ mile north of junction 1 of the M40, off the A40. Denham is also accessible by rail on Chiltern Railways, and there is a path linking the village to the station.
- **PARKING:** Car parking is available at the visitor's centre, although a charge is made. Parking, with picnic tables, is also available on the opposite side of the road.
- **LENGTH OF WALK:** $5\frac{1}{4}$ miles. Map: OS Explorer 172, Chiltern Hills East (GR 047865).

THE WALK

1. Start at the starburst of mosaics near the visitor's centre and turn right at the hedge. Go through two gates, crossing a road, and straight ahead through a third gate marked Coot Trail. On the far left you can see a line of red life preservers marking the route of the River Colne, and to your right the River Misbourne runs unseen. After crossing a charming bridge over the Colne (where you may see some of the aforementioned coots), you encounter a third waterway, the Grand Union Canal. On your left is Denham Deep Lock, where drinks and light snacks can be had at Fran's Tea Rooms, which also sells home-made chutneys.

2. Follow the towpath to the right, the Colne is now on your right as it weaves in and out of the canal. The towpath crosses onto the other side at the next bridge and then ducks under the roar of the A40. The canal

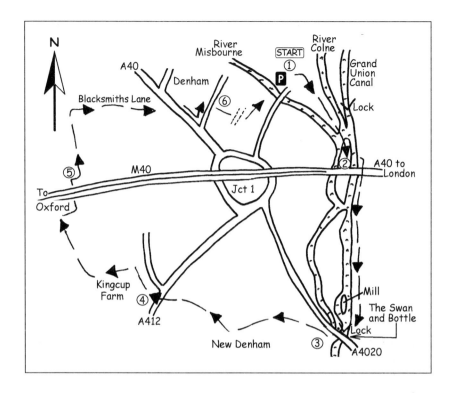

and river split to pass round an island, dominated by a featureless green building which is, in fact, a mill. There have been mills on this site for 1,000 years and this must surely be the most unsightly of the lot! Cross over the next bridge by Denham Marina and Uxbridge Lock. Just before the next bridge go into the car park for the Swan and Bottle and turn right onto the A4020.

3. Walk beside the island and then cross the road. About 200 yards down, the footpath turns left, just after the speed limit sign. Cross diagonally over an open space and into the backs of some houses. This is New Denham, a Victorian model housing estate, built in the 1870s by a local squire. On emerging from the housing, follow the footpath to the left and then right, towards Buckfield Farm. Just before the farm, the footpath heads left, signed to Rush Green. Go through a gate and follow the path until it dog-legs to the right at Southlands Manor and emerges on the busy A412.

4. Taking great care, cross the road and go down Willetts Lane opposite. Follow the road past Kingcup Farm and take the bridleway on the left after about 50 yards. A long straight stretch follows until you reach a junction of paths, at which you should go right over a stile. Cut across the field to the opposite corner and cross two more stiles – these are all part of the nine stiles mentioned earlier. There should be a hedge to your right and fruit trees to your left. Go over another stile, up a bit, and through a gate. Turn immediately right through some trees and over a couple of planks to emerge by a minor road next to Rush Hill Cottage. Turn left and over the busy M40.

5. Immediately after the motorway turn right down a made-up track. Just before it bends there is a stile and fingerpost marked Denham on the left. Take this and go over two stiles, the second of which sends you into the adjacent field. Go downhill under the shade of some mature oaks to a small stream and then up again, keeping the field boundary to your left, until you reach Blacksmiths Lane. Turn right down the lane and where it bends right continue straight ahead down a track; after a short distance take the footpath on the right, which heads towards a petrol station. Halfway along this path pass into the field on your right and aim for the gap between the garage and the house. On emerging from this alleyway turn right along the main road. Cross when it's safe and then turn left up the residential Cheapside Lane until you reach Denham Infants School on the right.

6. Follow the alleyway at the top of the school, past Denham Cricket Club's ground and the backs of some houses, until you emerge onto a minor road. Cross this and take the kissing gate soon after on your left into a meadow. Cut across this into the opposite corner and enter some woodland. Follow this round on the left until you reach the Misbourne again. Follow the river to a bridge which leads you to the back of the visitor's centre.

PLACES OF INTEREST NEARBY

Palmers Roses at Denham Court Nursery near Denham roundabout offers a spectacular sight from the road. It is a family run nursery that has been going for 50 years, specialising in both old and new types of rose, and their fields are open to the public at no charge during the summer months and between 9 am and 5 pm, except Sundays, for sales. Telephone: (01895 832035).

IVER AND THE SLOUGH ARM

A steady walk taking in rivers, a lake, and a canal.

The charming Little Britain Lake

Iver remains a well kept secret although many of us must have passed within a mile of it on numerous occasions travelling on the M25. The village's modern antecedents go back to Domesday Book, although there is evidence that man lived here in Neolithic times. Centuries of occupation have left their mark, including a church with an Anglo-Saxon window and a tower made of Roman bricks.

Built on a slight incline sloping down to the River Colne, Iver also sits near to Little Britain Lake. Part of a complex of lakes, this area has become a haven for wildlife. To the south of the village is the long and uncompromising Slough arm of the Grand Union Canal, a portion of which constitutes the heart of this walk. One of the last stretches of canal to be built, this waterway was constructed to carry Slough manufactured bricks into London, and to carry the capital's waste back to infill the old brick fields.

The Swan inn near the start of the walk offers an extensive set of both bar snacks and full meals. The pub's sloping beam roof and location on the corner of the village all lend to the creation of a traditional and friendly atmosphere, aided no doubt by the availability of Greene King and Courage beers, as well as a wide variety of wines. Telephone: 01753 655776.

- **HOW TO GET THERE:** Iver is on the B470 between Langley and Cowley, about 2 miles south-west of Uxbridge. It is also served by rail on the line out of Paddington. Iver should not be confused with its larger namesake Iver Heath, a few miles to the north.
- **PARKING:** Parking is available outside the shops on the High Street in Iver, or alternatively park on one of the many side roads.
- **LENGTH OF WALK:** 4³/₄ miles. Map: OS Explorer 172, Chiltern Hills East (GR 031831).

THE WALK

1. Start by the mini-roundabout near the southern limit of the village, opposite St Peter's church and near the Swan pub. Go down Swan Lane and through some white pillars. Go through the white metal gate where the road seems to begin to peter out and continue along a long straight stretch until the road bends to the left. Just before the bend, take the public footpath through a narrow gap on the right. Go over a stile, and the view opens out, although the path is flanked by wire fencing. At the next stile bear right onto a sandy track shaded by horse-chestnut trees.

2. You soon come to a gate that leads onto the gravel drive of Delafield Manor, an impressive, cream-coloured building, and Delafield Cottages, at the end of which there is a concrete bridge taking you across Colne Brook. Turn right and when you come to a road go up it and left over the M25. Follow the road as it bends down to the right, past Palmers Moor House and Farm to Iver Road. Cross the road carefully and go down the path immediately opposite. Two kissing gates sandwich a short avenue of trees at varying stages of maturity. On going through the second gate you face an attractive section of the River Colne.

3. Cross a wooden footbridge and you will come to a pretty weir around 40 feet wide. Stick with the river, ignoring the junction to your right and following a sign on a gate, inscribed 'London Loop'. Soon you will see Little Britain Lake with its distinctive willows on your left. Go

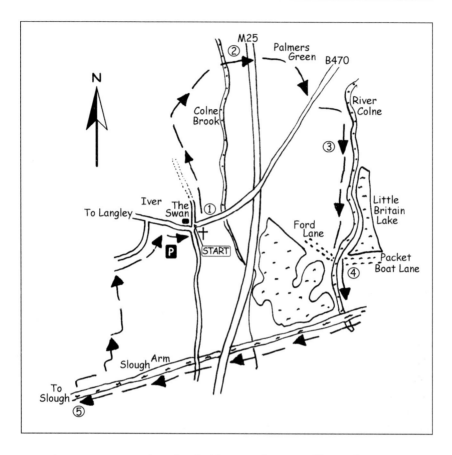

over two more wooden footbridges and you will reach a concrete bridge over the river that takes you to the lake. Leave the lake behind you and head over the top of Packet Boat Lane. This leads into the water for a good reason – it is a ford – and the road at the other end is known as Ford Lane.

4. A signpost here sends you straight on towards Stockley Park (3 miles away). The river is now on your right and narrows until it is almost totally congested by reeds. A small incline takes you to an iron bridge over the no-nonsense Slough arm of the GUC, a long straight stretch of canal. On the other side of the bridge, turn right, signed 'Beeches Way'. Further iron bridges carry you over the Colne and the Colne Brook and you also pass an old pillbox fortification on your left. Pass under the M25 and pass a mile marker at Thorney Lane Bridge.

The Swan Inn at Iver

5. Leave the canal at bridge 4 via steps made from old railway sleepers. Go left and left again over the bridge, and then immediately right on the other side towards the industrial estate. Hug the perimeter of the estate as it twists round, until you meet a three-way footpath marker. Take the left-hand turn and strike out across the field towards some housing, crossing an unmade road along the way. You come out by some garages and need to go up and then right, following the road round to the left until it reaches the local library and village hall. Turn right, following the main road over the mini-roundabout and back into the High Street. From here simply retrace your steps to your starting point.

PLACES OF INTEREST NEARBY

Black Park Country Park, a few miles to the north-west of Iver, is a sanctuary of peace and quiet in an increasingly built-up part of the county. Covering 530 acres, the park has woodland, grassland, and heathland as well as an impressive lake. Tucked away in the top right corner of the park is Pinewood Studios, and the park is often used as a location for feature films, including the Harry Potter series. Set walks, a lakeside café, and a children's play area all add to the attractions of the park. Telephone: 01753 734338.